Rudiments

K. J. Hannah Greenberg

Rudiments

Copyright ©2020 KJ Hannah Greenberg

All rights reserved. No part of this publication may be reproduced, distributed, or transmitted in any form or by any means, including photocopying, recording, or other electronic or mechanical methods, without the prior written permission of the publisher, except in the case of brief quotations embodied in critical reviews and certain other noncommercial uses permitted by copyright law.

Cover Art: KJ Hannah Greenberg

ISBN: 9798622940743

Seashell Books
www.myseashellbooks.com

Rudiments

Preface:

Relationships are blessedly commonplace. The manner in which each of us carries out negotiating, maintaining (and possibly dissolving) our connections, however, is bespoken. Consider that many communication scholars flounder when social climbing, and that many politicians, as well as other individuals possessed of great applied communication skills, tend to mess up romantic and familial links. What's more, most of us become so obsessed with the ways in which external points define us that we neglect our vital, intrapersonal comings and goings.

Rudiments explores much of this fuss. It jabs at the ways and means by which we coordinate our management of meaning with the conflicting voices in our heads and with the folks with whom we are involved. That is, this collection of poetry investigates how we get along with ourselves. It also investigates how we get along with others. While this book might romance the notion of sticking together, this book, simultaneously, makes no pretense that all liaisons are good; *Rudiments* espouses that some of our affiliations adversely impact our well-being.

To wit, while we struggle to reify ourselves over and again, sometimes, we succeed in making sense out of ourselves, and, sometimes, we succeed in making sense out of our associations with other people. Other times, we fail. Nonetheless, whenever we appreciate ourselves or our couplings, we discover that each amalgamation of cognitions and feelings are dissimilar. Hence, it's our distinct modes of handling self-talk and of handling conversations that ought to get celebrated. *Rudiments* strives to honor these particularities.

KJ Hannah Greenberg
Jerusalem, 2020

Rudiments

Lovers

Self, Family, and Friends

Nonintimates

Nature and Her Children

Unnatural Considerations

Introduction: Proportional Verse

Word.
Maybe more.
Three's increasingly better,
Although four makes friends.
Given unrestricted provisions, they multiplied,
Emulating hedgehogs singing under earthenware boxes.

Such foolish rhetorical discordances cast around,
Get stymied by calculating specialists,
Chewed until their meaning,
Oozes beyond canons.
Soon, expressiveness
Reeks.

Lovers

The Phenomenological Concept of the Body

Principally, the rheostat of lachrymose scavengers' revivifications,
Menacing, hastily skewed outlines, plus excited, epistemic longings,
Prove certain claims lack merits typically allotted to most vernal jobs,
To possibly confounding trifling groups, to unwisely bidden strictures.

Skin, cool and moist alike estuary sand, or hot like the winds of slayed
Furnetics, frequently vexes skills needed to master centrifuges' running.
Turkey basters, chinoises, ladles no longer behave as chosen playthings;
Similarly, pepper mills and pie birds befit lame bobs for tracheostomies.

An opposite possibility is overlords nullifying secret canards, silly goals,
Facing off against tavertine ruffians, disdaining supernatural adventures,
Disapproving: lumps of Terra Verde, fancy trussing needles, throw-outs,
Otherwise, we outgrow shiny shivs, limit okaying sharp edge propitiatory.

The phenomenological concept of the body, ever referencing corpuses plus
World, turns out to be an unhappy round where maturity-bound relationships
Wither. Contained by checks and balances' systems, pending epistemologies,
Various sets of "weather conditions" forestall inevitability, delay progression.

The Feminist Paradigm's no rationale for recent modesty or gaining gray hairs,
For nibbling tuiles (connections bring self-appreciation, which noises aloud and
Embraces zesters, creates complications, buffs mandolines, endures as suitable);
Human nature's collective adolescence aspires to shimmy, shake, else rock & roll.

That Photo, Which She Carried to Class

Along the speaking circuit of hillbillies, horrible monsters' swollen fingers,
Extrasensory abilities, flawed couplings, pimply noses, articulated opinions,
Shuttling pets to vets, pulling up springtime forbs, teaching herbal gymnastics,
Maybe, additionally, reserving castile soap for elders attending open schools,
A plethora of high manors, bards, and local serfs, reduced to sharing shrugs,
To smiling as throwing tantrums at morally relaxed others in Internet cafes,
Sought pink/gray beaches beneath Northeastern dumps, tiaras, gloves, oats,
Sleek modes of dress, suspicious manners (found in outdated bridal slicks.)

> That photo, which she carried to events, showed young beauty,
> Also free-flowing wisdom, lovelies hung on walls, gnawing
> On doors, climbing telephone poles; maidens with few fears
> Whose exploits included difficult pairings, full sublet prices.
> It radiated diatribes wrung out by oddly emotional teenagers,
> Depicts all forms of obsequious behavior, it reflected balance,
> Was spiced by: conflict, bravado, and the question of clean fun.
> As well, it previewed the rarity of reasoned decision-making.

Loosened onto existing ephemera, drunken gulls carry away bits of time, viscera,
Harnesses, latest careers amongst succulent barramundis, gasping tourists' limbs,
While records written by domestic divas parcel accidental excellence, split fifths,
Trumpet: dames' lingo, falsetto productions, women's song, acoustic guitar music.

Feminine health products never turn heads as long as people continue to be "smart
Enough" to discern twix glossy kinds of rhetoric or to be provoked into curiosity
Concerning manners of ingesting starfish, hunting quail, or gathering leprechauns.
(Folks oft iron minor inconveniences, yet contemplate the universe's complexity.)

Converse

I chanced a question,
At the wrong time.
The answer, an abhorrent little thing,
Plucked fresh off the vine,
Ushered forth greasy beasts, defanged,
But armed with unclotted civility.

Starlight, sunshine, watery reflections
Affect no allegiance toward gilded vows,
Fetch nothing, not sisters, from goodness.
Specifically, youth's straight stance quashes
Against routine wisdoms.

Spent gentleness squanders
Wishes, hopes, ambitions.
"Attraction" embodies "failure."
Night princes sup on blood.

Thereafter, mystique's radiant, diamond children,
Above reach, beyond accomplishment,
Sip sea shanties.

Whereas certain valleys protect mice,
They champion squirrels, harbor chipmunks.

Rightful spouses love because, not despite.

Measured Anguish at the Local Toadstool Malt Shop:
Take One

A scarcity of cobwebs confounded Erwan's attempted
Blending of linden leaves, under pressure, with ginger soda.
Hervey, all warts, slime, bulging eyes, plus patterned, speckled skin,
Coughed ahead of sucking down flies, espousing gossip, sipping watery ale.
Shortly thereafter, much earlier than sunset, music heralded Roparzh's arrival.

Gossamer wings, borrowed permanently from fair folk,
Attached with wire so fine as to be dangerous, also unsafe,
Enabled that eldritch gnome to float the copse's highest canopy,
Bow to budgies, bend near chaffinches, and stoop deeply to redstarts.
His rucksack warbled elfin symphonies, his toupee flagged avian waltzes.

The barkeep shrugged. Wormwort, an arsenic amber drop,
Moreover, handcrafted vitex ribbons, composed Aodrena's mix.
Most days, that glum-faced dwarf, betrothed petticoats, gala jewels, tears,
Forced smiles, awaited toothsome Yannic's thrust of gateway ferns, his footing,
Before she swallowed, kissed certain frogs, dusted off his cape, his boots, his cutlass.

Mostly, ogres, witches, angels, wolverines, harpies, failed;
None returned. Seasoned swords, fused conjuring, bloodied
Understandings, when choice, rose petal brew, arachnid-proofed,
Countermanded no steel's harmful aptitudes, undid no changelings'
Dark-fingered summons, restored no friend to nets, sweat, or breathing.

Rudiments

Awkwardly, Aodrena glugged for fey half as wide, twice as dainty,
Nodded ballads of King Cotentin vs. Duke Parterres. Her maiden songs
Sighed horses, armed units, goods culled alongside of mages, consigned,
Obliged, miserably caused to glamour rulers' heads, shapeshift soldiers, trap,
Honor kingdoms' duplicity via treacherous lost arts' old tricks, treason, fatigue.

Yannic, man at arms enough to enchant rhymes, additionally,
Heaved a great cudgel prior to pulling away from his bald-pated love.
No matter the gay, counted boughs directed toward their future fastening,
He traced battlefield wounds, viscera. She downed dewdrop draughts imbued
Heavily with valerian, lobelia, benzoin resin, alkalis surreptitiously dripped in.

Spiraling lifespans slip ringside, crumple in ordinary crucibles, not ever
Touch planned, proper enterprises, nor impact leaders' principled penury.
Perchance, likewise, scions of such unions descend toward suspicious acts.
Devoid of fiduciary improvement, land grabs, extra consorts, benefit, those
Winged nemesis, spectral soldiers, translucent corpses, set right all balances.

(Prescience, like butterflies, reads "toxic" or "bright."
Gloms won't be pushed aside to moss, toadstools.
War blades, alongside scrying, depose total peace.
Gilded glens rewrite no monsters as verdant tonics
Can't purchase concord; tippling just transfers woes.)

Measured Anguish at the Local Toadstool Malt Shop: Take Two

Cobwebs confounded Elias' attempts to mix
Linden leaves, under pressure, with ginger ale.
Hortance, warts, slime, bulging eyes, coughed.
(Gotham dude slurped up flies while waiting.)
Finally, melody announces Reginald's advent.

On gossamer wings, borrowed permanently,
Attached with wire so fine as to be chancy,
A pimpled gnome floats in from the canopy,
Bows to budgies, finches, sparrows, shares
Brooklyn Elvyn Symphony's seventh record.

Not just music blasts from his body pack; he oozes.
Tamsina shrugs. Wormwood's amber arsenic drops,
Also, a lidocaine ribbon brands his "pretty girl" mix.
Mostly, the she-dwarf, all betrothal petticoat curtsies,
Waits until Sylvester pushes aside the gateway ferns.

She dreams on sipping like folk half wide, twice dainty.
The war between King Filigree & The Duke of Arteries
Culls more than horses and men; it magics small people,
Transporting them to where gusts expand rulers' heads,
Where saltpeter bursts viscera of many valiant soldiers.

Young ogre gents, fairies, perhaps harpies, as well,
Fail to return from those far swords and conjuring.
No rose petal brews, no vials poofed by arachnids,
Can counterbalance cold steel's somnolent power.
Words, hearts, ardor, too, are helpless to avert loss.

Comely Sylvester knew violent, rhymed glamours,
Heaved cudgels too great for most bald-pated men,
But harvested no merriment, no timely fastening,
Only lingered viewing Alexis drink bitter draughts

Regurgitating those hours later in sorrow's puddles.
Valentines clandestinely pour staunch nothing.
Limitedly, at best, they cushion her prescience.
Elsewhere, honeys bleed the field, are trampled,
Skewered. So, she raises her glass to plutocracy
Somehow, staying herself from Anzid's pledge.

(Opting amnesia beneath fennel and toadstool,
Forgetting blakean scying, battle, love, death.
Tossing gilded scraps, ordering further freezes,
Attempting no purchase of new comrades, not
Dreading draggling, blood-crusted vestments.)

A Meadow Morning's Limitations

"Good morning, fair shepherdess,
How grow the forbs on yonder hill?"

"Rightly, good shepherd, sir,
I must attend my large flocks, still."

"Ah, my bonny, golden lass,
The wind, the sheep, the April wine."

"True, fine shepherd, sir,
Springtime greens the local vine."

"Regard! Butterflies, buttercups, I
Witness these worldly glowings."

"Aye, yet my lambies cry,
Their mames stray far, amowing."

"The dales, they are afilling up,
The clover, it's anodding.
The robins sing, 'fore taking wing,
Those fey folk are aplotting."

"Wait for me by yonder tree,
There, branches screen sun play."
I'll watch you step, without romance;
'tis what my mama doth say."

"Silly bud, look, the earth's ablooming."

"Wise sir, look— my ewe needs grooming."

"Forget the fleece, let's make peace
Come, waltz along with me, now."

"Just you jump and spin, without that grin,
Or you'll make due among your cows."

I Gave You Me

I embraced a quite wonderful dream!
'til I awoke to find the scene a fantasy,
A crystal bubble, a mere crafted shell,
Fabricated delight, fantastic dell, failed
Design of a sketch wrought carefully;
I gave you me. I gave you me.

We rolled our bodies often, in tune
With no harp music, promises' song.
My heart, better than skipping stones,
Counting pages, wrinkles, mornings,
I'd wish you health, I'd wish me love.
Fancying we'd sail away.

Your sweat and hair, mosaic-like
Swayed in mortise and tendon
On sky-covered beds, while sun
Chilled me, blurred your face,
'til all I had gifted was gone,
All wonder sucked from me.

Lotus Feet

With me hobbled, you sailed, knowing my frisson when dreading abandonment.
Our hectcrodyne loving, black and blue marking of attachments without Velcro,
Got built by dirks caroming my guts, shaving my viscera, important bits sinking.
You churl. You boor. Lotus feet aren't adornment, not endearment, but crippling.

Dreaming, I still run like horses, transverse vales where inoffensive dear ones,
Hidalgos all, provide succor, ovular safety, offer up friendly scrum. There, no
Imprimatur of duplicity roots me. No ravening, unkind predator predominates.
Themes of great consequence separate prey from assailant, divide you and me.

Ineluctable expression repairs no knee injuries, restores no zithers' function,
Creates no family unity, draws no diamonds. It's uncontentious to maintain
That a skirt, which I adored, followed entirely from porphyry; I spoke purple
Tulips. Woe to beasts! Not all red crystals are igneous; some bleed naturally.

Tomorrow's Bleak,
Worry-Woven Landscape

Tomorrow's bleak,
Worry-woven landscape,
Radiates your mystique.
My troubles mistaken,
We pursue lighter peaks.

Such smiles enhanced,
By your starshine nights.
Your continuous glance,
Heats with careful kindness,
Lifts me clear of romance.

Daisy meadows, drizzly
Woods, too, yield, proclaim
Morning. As evening's grief
Disperses, I glory your name,
Your warmth. My hope grows.

In return, you must need
Me. Beauty and skylight
Mingle. The sun follows
Varying twilight steps,
Grants kisses thereafter.
Frees.

Contemporary Coupling (a Ballad)

Two gals decked in ribbons,
Some gents sporting tails.
Went swirling 'round the dance floor,
'til the women swapped their males.

Hi de hi ho,
Hi de hi hee,
The russet one's
The man for me.

My partner spoke in riddles.
That link, he ragged my brain.
He answered but a little,
So I'd seek him again.

Hi de hi ho,
Hi de hi hee,
The russet one's
The man for me.

We talked 'til the new sun,
Floated up the sky.
My resistance became undone
(He was a clever guy.)

Hi de hi ho,
Hi de hi hee,
The russet one's
The man for me.

Next, we supped together,
Strolling, shopping, all the same.
My code was growing thinner,
While I hardly knew his name.

Hi de hi ho,
Hi de hi hee,
The russet one's
The man for me.

My best girl, she said love was
Coloring my cheeks.
She pointed out a single cause,
Though we'd coupled just a week.

Hi de hi ho,
Hi de hi hee,
The russet one's
The man for me.

A fortnight, still together,
The russet one and I.
I might last near forever,
With this the red-haired guy.

Hi de hi ho,
Hi de hi hee,
The russet one's
The man for me.

Midas' Touch

'Ol Roper,
My weasel-chasing dogbit,
Toted home THIS PRODUCT
Wrapped pretty.

THIS PRODUCT makes muscles,
Produces magnetism
Enhances personality, so
Ma's picture magazine promises.

Clementine, my darling, packed,
Lost and gone forever.
I kept THIS PRODUCT;
Paupers ain't need no queens.

Pleasant Wishes, Little Kisses

Pleasant wishes, little kisses, kittens, puppies, fish,
Tender whispers, vined Septembers, grand hormonal itch.

Antiquated pledges, posies soldiered straight in tiny rows,
Bottles, powders, fursty pizza pies, pairs of uncovered toes.

Sailing past some bits of heart, flecking a few landscapes,
Skipping over leaks, longings, smarts, seeking cheap escapes.

Pairing's long been oversold as an answer to nights' woes
Yet, fun, solace, other salves, need spring from separate prose.

Fortuitous Wanderings

Silent, lime-colored worms slither,
Scale silk meant to wake sulking monsters;
Webs shimmer when witnessing certain morbidity.

Dark days, rain clouds gather,
Push boys plus girls to huddling,
Fill university halls with rank puddles.

Scrupulous brides face away,
Ignore photographers' prompts to pirouette,
Choose, instead, smileless, shadowed portraits.

Unpleasant gifts stay stacked,
Remain ribboned reminders of celebrations,
Forced upon oboe soloists who miss high C.

Adult Wibbling, Wobbling, Falling Down

Adult wibbling, wobbling, falling down, starting all over is droll.
Concurrent with urging boys and girls, even unicorns, to grow up,
So much fussing over next generation's stuff makes elders forget
Some unwilling censorship of sacred familial information byways.

Yes, sewing pockets into the cape folds of grotesque actors, evokes
Patterns in lesser places than marked ridges induce in buffalo hide.
Also, fictions' alleged empirical framing of problems remains tosh
Media coverage–enthralled people willingly rely on writers' edges.

Whenever reading about infamous metropolises, in glossies or online,
It no longer suffices to skip electronic curses; delusive data's popular.
Perhaps, veiling broadcasts' chroma could help amigurumi reproduce.
Failing such strategies, there's always old, foolish auditors' opinions.

My Mister (a Didactic)

When you rise,
Greet horizons with your eyes.
Should it rain,
Green weather washes out your pain.
We watch the same sun, feel watery kisses
Over leagues we remorse, similarly we miss.

When you wash,
Laugh your bubbles toward my place
When you comb,
Smile the curls around your face.
We both sheath, obscure with cloth,
Press against knit, cover our loss.

Seasons cycle, spin.
Spring calls charm your way
Fancies firm manly whims.
Remember me this day

When you dine,
Drink your fill, ale binds,
When you play,
Be fair, be good, beseech.
Stay stout of heart
Ask health, ask joy, pray smart.

A span's fermentation,
A week's careful keep,
A time's resolution,
All dream-woven sleep.

Daisy thoughts,
Torch lit greetings,
Stars conspire
Toward kingdoms' meeting.

I love you!
Sentiments' parameters,
Bind, do tie my tongue
'til nothing matters
Still, peonies grow, persevering,
Previewing a distant springtime.

Silver Moss Fingers

Silver moss fingers hang
Against banded trunks.

Also, golden thoughts of leaves,
Those sunlit yellow diamonds, sway.

WordStar music, such as never seeps,
Bringing angels' tears inlaid with frost.

I was rich, too, when I pressed
Against your iridescent skin.

Some ends, interwoven in space,
Glitter like worn party favors.

There's much "chew and spit" in close examinations.
Cultural contracts reveal many matchmaking patterns.

Akin to childbirth, coupling
Usually suffers seven places of travail.

Love is dandelion seeds, muddy frogs,
Always sweet sucklings' sleep.

Thereafter, strawberry highs, glycemic joy,
Curve to costume extra words.

Flattery possesses limited charms.
There remains no alternate to Eden.

Falling Cradleless through Spring's Evening Boughs

The woman abided by the spring's evening boughs,
Was wowed when zephyrs took sides with hummingbirds.
Such tones, audible gossamers, were dandelion parachutes,
Suitably montaged, drifting clear of old laundry, hedge clippings.

Chippering bands wondered where his head next graced,
Facing sunset-hued beauties, jetting off, skittering her reach.
Teaching nothing of acceptance's better pathos. Why try flying
From cradles; more than crashing resounds infidelity's screech.

Peaks of "drug-resistance" choices spun harder, faster. A measure
Later, his pleasure transformed not as trophies or quests, but thin ego
Dribbles tickling all manners of verities. Moonlight's sleepless howls,
Bower-ridden, anyway, might have suddenly sired rapid self-penalties.

Wee breezes, nocturnal gusts, called forth alternate forms, wore down
Moments where lust melted hallow. Dreams denied, fascinations settled.
Mettle, mores, political correctness, make no difference to certain tramps,
Like him, a husband/father intent on leaving panty trails on urban hillsides.

Passing Thoughts (a Carol)

My passing thoughts linger, frame you
Love's snapshots flicker in review.

Your equation's call abided,
Certain others get divided,
By Ergo's links, lull's quieted,
Sums' mutuality's construed.

Heart-spots flourish, occasions find,
Voices' rub simple, speeches bind,
Miles rules, but thoughts entwine,
A whisper joins us, bridges two.

My passing thoughts linger, frame you
Love's snapshots flicker in review.

Across plateaus our words did dance,
Now fused by sight, motes spurred romance,
Your nod, your smile, your special glance,
Animate, give phonemes their due.

Distance jumped, our fingers touch,
They link, they hold, they reach to clutch,
We grope, we grab, we "talk" as such,
Grand moments these, our pair's renewed

My passing thoughts linger, frame you
Love's snapshots flicker in review.

Kowtowing to Social Fads:
A Tragic Romance

If viewers saw gushing, they'd be dismayed,
Pay minimum for such designated meddling,
Insofar as the high-flying lady had forgotten
Mawkishness putrefies airwaves' personages,
Plus regularly contributes cultural weirdness,
Catches links to more verdant lives than hers.

Being sagacious, he weighed and measured
Disruptive antics, allowed schemes to swing,
Let fall hardly any truly subjective ambitions.
Rather, he directed microphones, computers,
Audio equipment for her exclusive pleasure,
While he overwrote code, paid editors extra.

After donning her chime-laced cap, snatched
From a previous release party, she mustered
Consolation from her Snapchat hangers-on.
The smart bells/whistles of his construction,
Anyway, intervened, only deactivated by his
Private channels, which she charily avoided.

In lieu of broadcasting wholly pure attributes,
Polysemic perspectives, sparkling cordierite,
Moonstones, parures, gold dust, refinement,
She revised termagant, sapphires, old civility
Up until her soporific management mangled
The couple's soon-to-be-mediated romance.

He deliberated forever forgoing viable efforts,
Hiring some not-at-all-surreptitious detectives,
Dumping exploding crowds for hobo alliances.
Finally, while in self-enforced semi-isolation,
Bottles of stuff helped him to move his mind
Elsewhere, anywhere, another place from her.

As Obsessions Do

As obsessions do, it grew.
Pink spring clover, wild carrots,
Natural bridal paraphernalia, also
Plantain, bladed leaves, barbed fields,
Breakfast. Heart break.

As miasma does, it was.
Conformity without regard,
Procrustean manners,
Dottle-coated ewers,
Otherwise indirect folly.

As ambition could, it would.
Form spiny, dense, furze-like,
Excessive contraptions, then
Shape glittery echelons higher
Before routing compassion.

The Physical that was You

Red and gold flags, the physical that was you.
Not day lilies, purple pansies, sunup bird call.
Rather, softly slapped bareback rides,
Interspersed gold nuclide, plutonium,
Bed sheets in July, balloons, tinsel,
Warm sleep.

Today's conversation failed with flourish.
Our discutable rickety dipper clattered.
Became monkey faces, moist at night,
Arcade miracles, time card tallies,
Calculated matchbox ponies,
Ichor, etiolate fronds.

Today is Forever
Tomorrow's Twice Yesterday

Today is forever tomorrow's twice yesterday.
When we kneeled together, yearning for strokes,
But daring just whispers, remaining chaste, not
Touching, I lied; lifestyle disparities did matter.

As bonhomie girls' candy hearts signify "barely me;"
It's more the pity perfidious sorts get rich, die young,
Never suffer manias concomitant to ordinary living,
Nor fashion feasible, literary cohesiveness in a row.

See, elders in aboriginal cultures seek appendages' fail.
They climb floors, wedge boxes, maybe heed old lectures.
To them, not degrading locals counts. Eventually, agony,
Also retribution, balances condoning irredeemable acts.

Nestled in gift boxes, leather purses painted with sunset,
Become flotsam lapping at shorelines, raising questions.
Gormless passersby rubberneck pangolins' tawdry junk.
Gobbledygook rests in the compendia of social treatises.

Elsewise, wazzocks, fully contrary, uncover hocus pocus,
Play at self-reinforcing gaolers, bite testable explanations.
Gossips bare prodromes' realities, argument psychpomps.
Alternate collusions, abet underwriting genotexts' outlays.

Given car accidents, cancer, also spiraling costs of living,
Besides a grand increase in socially probated malfeasance,
Golden agers cease believing anyone will endure evermore.
Realize, cultural jabber often postures everyone as "artists."

So, it's left to our round robin recitals to bring home truth.
Folks, those unable to leap past ageism, get stymied again.
Conflicts in research palaces can't remove broken plinths.
Sometimes, breathing snow globes' air goes very wrong.

Asiatic Arecas

Asiatic arecas, all lambent in the sun,
Tall stepstools to celestial balls,
Inclusive treetops to a one,
Bring a susurrus of social gaffes.

We snigger at adolescent acts,
At glugging, snorting, plus igniting.
We point at awkward dramas' casts
Stare toward shy jilliken girls.

If plinths, glasses, mallets would not whirl,
Not twirl like merry-go-round riders,
There'd be no fear of injury, no trees birled;
Just here, there, somewhere, baffled denizens.

So to modern party scenes, such gatherings, amen.
Pugnacity among glittery, costly, confettied props,
Brings quandaries now and then, whenever
Great, healthier behavior models seem lacking.

Certain friends console hosts' hacking
Desired old peacemaking skills,
Offer up cajeput's or weed's backing
To keep secret all their fun.

Patterning with Holes

Openwork fabric, patterned with holes, like many friendships,
Adds zing, zest, notice, accent, perhaps oomph to life's dailies.
Whereas gold oak leaf might not be necessary for most courses,
Needle plus thread, together, attach fruits, fancies, fantasies, fun.
Turned from bone, bobbin lace, that amply detailed paraphernalia,
Fine ground, outlined archetypes, reminds us small matters count.

Anything that keeps us tatting the knots, loops, threads of exchange
Makes us join, continue on, harmonize, recognize, use conversation,
Potentially, arranges dissimilar filaments, while enticing, ensnaring,
Noosing us to showy, nearly attractive ways, means, routes of union.
Contemplate that diaphanous, "wedding ring fine" heirloom knitting,
Joy-fashioned, embellished memories, ornate filaments, fuses persons.

Really, contemporary, chemical similitudes, although fully mechanized,
Suggest essential heritage, yet linger, thereafter, bereft of pure harmony,
Original sparks, or companionship build from silk, bliss, bullion, silver.
Simple fees purchase no lasting love. Synthetic decorations wind zilch.
Per whitework, recall deletions, damage, irrespective of old embroidery.
Routing designs through hoops, hamster wheels, culls flaws, fault, folly.

In balance, not all ribbon becomes Chantilly; some folks descent together
Without ever touching, without sharing words. They struggle hours, years,
Long since having surrendered mature values. Larking, instead, indefinite
Curios as so much jumbled pettiness, reasons to fight, to enlarge distances.
Successfully fostering compassions demands accounting of fibers, twists,
Finishes. Sloppy handling best results in lovers knots; worst, in loose ends.

Self, Family, and Friends

Can I be Rare, Too?

If you are rare, can I be rare, too?
In less time than needed to braid keychains,
I could perch on spikes, like Australian thorn birds,
Thrust off sufficient self-perceived "embarrassments,"
As to change, rather than to terminate, our relationship.

Skipping along the periphery of glabrous greens (grown with ill cause),
I could also rubrice sharp passages as filled with "ease and light." Forfend
That midife's mandate keeps our critical courses accessible via locked spaces.
Only give hatchling promises or passing seasons (those met during earlier spans),
 I would appropriate unpronounceable microscopes for calculating tarantulas' fangs.

Conjuring up make-believe monsters does naught for dancing mortise and tendon.
Dunderdoodles, blue-tongued skinks, plus vegetarian "meatballs," all sometimes burn.
Better to fail at placing staid beckets overboard or to sink incorrigible rhinos with wine,
Than to intertwine in amusement park lagoons ordinarily intended for reducing: salads
To sessile, single forms to dress rehearsals, generations to plastered attributes, coughing.

Lately, some of my literary pas de deux, those irregularly curbed,
Invoked: predator memories, more successful communications, plus
Swollen breasts, swiffers' replacements, satin-lined toppers, unidirectional
Enchantments, second person POVs, jubilee fools, sufficient emotional forecasts.
Always keep in mind that telling a woman you "love her" is never, ever, ever, ever enough.

Salivating away Tension

I.

TMJ aches across my jaw, while
My tongue lolls among roustabouts.
The sun's unevenly fallen to shadows,
Where .50 caliber cartridges loop shoulder-belts.

Racked teeth roll clockwise, then back, as
Saliva shoots, leaks, again, during mud season.
Individuals, bent on destroying UFO sightings,
Hint at saltwater crocodiles, court local loutishness.

Sibilance of poverty, racial hatred, maybe
Produces spans of random Lukumi visitations.
Good girls slip away, shake heads, thumb home;
Everyone else employs violent language, achieves rot.

In separating from smarmy YouTube stills,
We forget kibble, overlook fashioning congeniality.
Narrow ways, even now, make lane changes challenging,
Rough up commuters intent on fumbling into ordered lines.

Additionally, resources available to middle-aged
Parents, won't account for creative, alternate activities,
Increased vocabulary in healing skills, marzipan body parts,
Mortgages on plumbers' vacation condos, swarms of mental critters.

II.

No matter the resolute apologies,
Chasing adolescents to college is stupid.
Hacking iPhones, too, like fixing keyboards,
Brings only sophomoric gestures, faux gold leaf.

Theatre crew parties, alternatively,
Riotous urban glitter, hand built flower pots,
Literary works gummed up with unnatural modesty,
Glum envisionings, snails, become "correct," not popular.

Supplementary problems, beyond street level, past
The guy with his hand out, the rabbit hole, the maze,
Concerning denizens familiar with Varangians, often stop
Along with shields deflecting unwelcomed, semiprivate reviews.

Allegedly, folks in cahoots with mirandized
Rodents lynch journalists, buy dangerous curricula,
Sprinkle entire episodes of NGO field agents, kiss pit bulls,
Shred sports coaches, share youth villages, & twiddle nose hair.

Scholarship could compensate tension after
Juicy jowls silence certain sorts of reptilian hatchlings.
Until such time, indicated chamberlains' frustrated attempts
To gather bits fallen against kin, at best, get spat or licked away.

Shedding

Tears swim down, gumming sides, making room for crescendoing bravuras,
Until weary epiglottises becomes incapable of throwing off chaff. Rectified
Souls find access to apexes, become rewoven of essential stuff, concurrent
With the rest of us trying to ooze thanks for essentials, but getting stymied.

It's not merely life's avoirdupois, but also complete pieces of silent gratitude,
That continue as entirely devoid of formation's splendor. Those bits, derived
From bad addresses, burnt letters, mistaken memories, other claptrap, cheapen
Mediunity, weaken miracles, suck power from paranormal phenomena, sadden.

Strange habits repeatedly suppress spiritual immunities, without recompense,
Leave actors not corporally sick, but dying of other salts, bases, also bitters.
Such remarkable chunks deprive, moreover, children of whirly-twirly rides,
Extract dedicated ticks of imperative living from everyone, including elderly.

Later, associates' good intensions are of no assistance, fashion not any solace
Since the remnants of high end evolutions droop like saggy ears, used tissues.
(Too many folk resort to hanging their heads from car windows, breeding lice,
Posing as furries, running from remorse's comfort, fleeing sorrow's potency.)

No grimoires exist for atonement. Loathing taints penitence as long as deeper
Resentments run free. "Regular" doctors, too, work useless even as we refuse
The Greatest Healer, partner beside ill-conceived notions, bloat our collective
With amuse bouches fashioned from duplicity or other astringent conjectures.

While we want to be jake with The Boss, to be enfolded, if not for eternity,
At least twelve months, in forgiveness, in tenderness, furthermore accord,
Almost always, we neglect projecting details until discovering that nuance
Constitutes the fill of salvation, the core of recovery, and significant balm.

Life's woods, hedgerows, lakesides don't lack beneficent spots or sunshine.
Rather, some of us have strayed so far as only select vesicles, merely precise
Vessels show utility, potentially free us, limit transgressions, shiv Heavenly
"Permission" to restore health, to loosen our command of disturbing baggage.

The strong charges counter to our names fade only if and when and whether
We believe we're capable of change, of constitutional rarity, of having some
Caustic consequences reversed, of letting go, yielding, of losing ownership
To the Master Videographer who wants to employ calm filters to our films.

Personal Journeys

Personal journeys, arising from inside wilderness,
Elevate individuals by dint of pushing apart fears
To travel alongside dark, repulsive, weird ground,
Until shadows, pressures, pain, exhaustion dispel
(Courage, foolishness, some combination thereof,
Change wanderers hazarding vexing adventures.)

No matter the ends, such explorations yield takers
All manner of self-discovery, buried truth, wisdom.
(By churning souls constructively, taxing exploits
Temporarily fashion frustration, add illusory loss)
Prior to actualizing the better measures of "good."
Likewise, they compel exacting spiritual changes.

Redemption generates persistent empowerment
Builds fiber past "good enough" reasons' alibis.
(See, core expeditions are labor-intense, arduous,
Require quiet bravery, loud acceptance, fidelity.
We need intentional or accidental flying beyond
Built up worries, deterrents to growth, despair.)

Body, Salubrious: An Unexpected Visitor

I ooze. Sometimes blood, maybe viscera, occasionally gelatinous substances, blossom,
Bud from extremities, grow a tail, actualize my personal agglutination, postprandially.
A few offerings appear before meals, elsewise, nights, during eclipses or pulpy shows.

Meanwhile, mellifluous passages, snatches of tones plus their siblings, chime four-four time,
Echo ship halls, direct waves, seal sour notes in exacting ringing, tooting, clanging, pealing.
Those simple breaks from silence, along with paw prints, evidence my internecine struggle.

Excluding me, no survivors sail the starry dark, look into nothingness, fashion fear, awe,
New formations crave exceptional resources. I repossessed their drogues quite long ago.
Eventually, when my bones transmute to dust and my flesh sits wasted, I'll morph again.

Sail Away

Sail away. Help me, please. Release.
Tease others. Let me go. You know my tact.
My sighing eye. My tears, fears, jubilation.
Nightmare lullabies. Keepers' games;
All the same kinds of ugly. Dull moments
Spent bright and clear on glens, dells,
Hillsides near, dear, precious in sunlight.

Trees align, rows by rivers, copses filling
Landscapes. Shivering, I drape leaves, forbs,
Orbit your rays. Shadowy secrets persist;
Bloom in mist's fine droplets. Pristine no more,
Monsters loom. Here, there, elsewhere.
Mechanisms, gears, punked out garbage,
Streams funky music beyond bayou bedrock.

Sock fabrics stretch. Wovens yield,
Speed along limbs, toward maverick
Explanations. Lamely pitch forward.
(Taming monkeys causes moonshine,
Weed, plus speed to multiply). High
Hopes of dope call forth authorities.
Nope, ain't 'gonna run away home.
Nope, ain't 'gonna run away home.

HaPupakim (Belly Button)

I have a little hollow,
It sits beneath my waist
And when I shake my tummy
It moves within its space.

What is this little debit?
Is this some teenage dream?
Look closer now, don't shy away;
It's my hapupakim.

Some Boats

Some boats, sailing seas,
Encircle others' POVs,
Until drawn against.

Great Veils of Regret

Great veils of regret drape my sight,
Fear palls me, so afraid you might
View my mantle. I know that bright ways,
Illustrious days are your preferred cape.

Yet, should happiness' fabric cinch me,
I would grow less radiant. Perceive,
Although this gown glistens, such plumage,
Bars my vision, burns a nub scarcely risen.

Crocus Friends

Crocus friends blossom suddenly,
Usually becoming vibrant after storms,
But wither when too much sun reminds
Us that good weather dethrones winter.

Pregnant with Joy

Banners of happiness slip, iridescent nacre,
Between aureate columns, muguet de bois,
Pikaki. Our personal adytons prove great
When hearts' private greenhouses prevail.

Consider wooly-muzzled, wild ponies,
Brinking on iridule thresholds, sniffing
Freedom, chuffing 'til somnambulating
Wastrels, (vertigo countenance), guffaw.

Rarely, given heliotrope, are feral letters
Assembled, strung together from outland
Sentiments, seasons beyond snowflakes.
Fragrant mauves bloom no haptic answers.

Inimitable nature flowers sporadically,
Causing enriched grownups to entangle
In citreous parallels, to commit beauty,
To struggle free, to collect hierophants.

Most snows fall in soft, white platelets.
After hills darken, precious few auras
(or triptychs of the same), can continue;
Stygian industries, pulp, feathers, raid.

Regrettably, "affection" means "date
"Rape," "glaciation's Marengo Phase."
Some periods of peroration's elevation,
Prove not magic, quiet, or restorative.

Myth's revered locates, unexpectedly,
Calm. Scaling sky-crowned mountains
Stays dangerous. Canines jeopardize.
Central heating does break repeatedly.

Beyond most conurbations' clinics,
Fancies create everlasting presences
Sufficient to redefine "providence."
Elsewise, foppish valiants eke it out.

Readings, book launches, conferences,
Pledge not returning to quislings' bounty.
Everyday word worlds perchance comber
More than transportation ought demand.

Budding apart, great truth tellers
Float grand depths on vital issues,
Lose weight, hold smart phones,
Grow no exhilaration or gravidity.

Returning to Egypt with a Clean Lute

I believe in heroes and nickelodeons, shyamalaned goings-on,
Stocking stuffers, yellow violets, scapulas used as paperweights.

See, recycling typing papers, buying rugose dogs, rewriting, over again,
Sijos, plus remembering to breathe whenever sitting on quaggas, are good.

Revisiting steam tunnels, though, rots. Trial by fire, at most ivy-type colleges,
Leaves out overpasses, invites vexatious buddies, excludes functional syllabaries.

Subsequently, ill-tuned heckle phones, sanguine monsters, coruscating dungeons,
Starry nights, opossums, random wage workers, all posture as sublimated beauties.

Buskers, perennially agitated, agonize (their tattered salwar kameez notwithstanding).
They know that many adolescents' day care providers fashion bilkis, consume weed.

Cognitive limits imposed by cartouches, concordanced information, carry on as stale.
Mathematical concision, dirty laundry, junket pots still deprive childhood innocence.

Few grasp that protecting the young matters; violetwood, as impressed upon by bores,
Unless dried or oiled, produces an abundance of enceinte. Confervae sprout tendrils.

Runny viscous substances, too, as determined by librarians, scatter precious treens.
Most times, collections of indolent lizards lose value, deny academic desperation.

Pulp remains literature's costume jewelry, slimy wind instruments, repeatedly,
Befriending none, not wild ducks, not tenured deans, not even piebald ponies.

Had I Wishes

Had I wishes, they'd not be used on wings,
On super powers, other synthetic things.
Given millions, I'd save for infirm years,
Evading magic, also surplus social fears.

Yet, balloons collapse. Friendships, like ours, deflate.
Some provedores cease sending sweethearts telegrams,
Substitute with unripe ackee, likewise toxic elderberry,
Determine the need to mark how we think, speak, act.

Morally relaxed hearts then meter out gestures or roses,
Hankies, sugar, give bad reviews, unequivocal critiques.
Assume levels of love, longing, destiny, also obligation.
Skewer fairytales, communicate unfortunate narratives.

It seems, your mothers, all ebullient, lethal cassava,
Educated your womenfolk, to hastily throw sprigs
(samphire plus parsley.) Those ballistics, honed at
Right angles, mean to dissuade daughters-in-laws.

Holiday Clothing

Young smiles in women's bodies, my daughters,
Beg money for holiday outfits, hair ribbons, shoes.

While counting out paper and coin, I think how we hope forgiveness, fast,
Complete, cost free clemency for penchants grown from former gildings;
Acting insouciantly, wronging many people, conjecturing gossip, audibly,
Daring to believe that denial might actually be fungible for base behavior,
Inviting minimalization, its twin, rationalization, random sorts of blather.
Plus, encouraging habituated busybodies to pull caricatures out of teapots,
Even as forgetting to "hide" strayings, or enroll spheres of accountability.

It's funny, perhaps sad, folks perceive gross errors as simple traffic accidents.
Truth, though, evidences our incomplete efforts at adopting excuses' children.
Bad things, wound on imagination's best costumes, remain choices not easily
Rectified, now, then. Notwithstanding spates of bowing, swaying, prostrating,
Moaning, crying, every disillusionment sticks. Not bolts, trusses, man-mades
Save. Sure, we can elect to delay ('til half way 'round the year) all atonement.

Although sfarims' small steps invite change, discern 'twix fiction and verity,
Tweak us, fell juvenile understandings of timeless narrations, of adaptations,
We stay surprised when various gifts linger undeveloped, when devastation
Buds like almond blossoms, when life's rigors prove exhausting. Discipline,
Heavenly help remains altogether compulsory for settling the uninhabitable.

Meanwhile, my daughters stand secure, absolved, released.
Unwrapping such articles as I could never choose.

Their holidays bound forward brightly, colorful, light-filled.
No lack of splendor detours their steps.

The girls' mirrored credit, like new skirts, fresh blouses, matching
Socks, proliferates easily in their days, their nights, their dreams.

To such youth, fasting is as feasting is as festive dancing.
Celestial music sings them. They experience peace.

Their futures strum with grace, with uncommon concord.
Specifically, they're okay with offering amends.

This year, maybe, I, too, will get new garments. I'll recognize trees' silhouettes
At dusk, breezes, birds, sunshine. I'll celebrate praying by quorum, sit outside
After services, accede to our leaders with wonder, smile at other women, voice
"Thanks" more often. Perhaps, it's actually that my domicile's irreproachable,
My life's as it is supposed to be, in spite of my obstinate connections to flaws.

My moments, on balance, no matter their ilk, might, in fact, be integral. My
Deeds, too, might illuminate. My tears may well fill angels' cups, may bring,
Before the grandest throne, a measure that possibly appears as acceptable, as
Passable for a twelve month span and my words, perchance, will prove good.
Maybe, this evolution, I'll experience no customary ripping before restoring.

A renewed maiden, I'll know no incendiary rending before rebuilding,
No painfully rigorous scribbling out. My bad spots will just jettison.

I finger dress fabric. My girls trust. They have confidence in good as "good,"
As well as that the Otherworldly Scribe is compassionate, merciful, kind.

After Twenty Years, Towels Fray

After twenty years, towels fray, limnae creatures also wonder water's worth.
Invisible hedgehogs' hibernacula, alongside many kinds of relaxed editors,
Begin despising sassafras roots, fairy wings, wee pieces of acorn pancakes,
Even as strutting beside thoughtful streams of binturong fur, solved shouts,
Thunder, lightning, electrical squalls, Photoshopped regoliths, tooth decay.
Critters yearningly gaze at yesterday's métier while all eyes go chalcedony.
Dogs, maybe hyenas, purple smoke, kaleidoscope cries, dead moths clinch
Self-determination shown by "abuse survivors," "pets," "wise pensioners."

Consider, at street level, various costermongers shout bananas and cherries.
I'd take that from their barrels had you not insisted on boutique affections.
Hence, I sufficed through bull fiddles though my loving needed mandolins.
I wanted to acquiesce to ordering in Chinese noodles, to acquiring guquins,
To run around buck naked, except for an old kimono lent by our concierge.
Rather, you recalled antiques' costs, granted no restrictions on private parts,
Esteeming that principles of intimacy exist as they do, especially officially.
Further hazarding ions with unpaired spins might fetch paramagnet powers!

Until tomorrow, more harmatttans blowing toward New York convey trash.
Babble fishes resume divulging multi-linguistic laconic expressions, mirth.
Mustelids organize blues bands, red specks, green-marked shells, conscript
Insect warriors, casually. Later, do orient themselves in thermal holocausts.
School clerks continue calling fathers to request kids' field trip permissions.
Secret suns saunter together with polarly matched elements as splendorous
Spots (known for ferule reinforcements) abandon rest to slumbering rustics.
Motorcades, jazz clubs, elephants, blithely disregard their mestizo heritage.

After all, burying troubles in haymows, reveals moist places where tree bits
Harbor leafy brightness, makes sebaceous most sugar-coated examinations.
Relationships evolve epigenetically, unstructured eggs plus wiggly sperms
Cause potential; when truth churns public potholes, it skips when kneeling.
In toxins, nations leapfrog through forests, Oenomelian lakes. Algonquins
Dance, end purposeless ballet sessions, dispose aebleskivers, displace 'em.
Yet, informed choices allow guidance, cease erasure, sidetrack cenotaphs,
Row in daisies, got trod upon by emotional peacocks (liaisons take work.)

Generations of Morning Glories:
Dialoging a Changing Mother/Daughter Relationship

Quick maturity, in motherhood, allows for twining habit plus attractive blooms,
Likewise, a tolerance of rigorous circumstances. Morning glory's vast tessitura
Remains despite her fragility of flowers, the sum rapidity with which she dies.

"Hold my hand, do smile at me,
Sip the vial of life with me,
Be my friend a time with me,
Please stay around a while."

Much energy gets consumed teaching kids to selectively invest, to choose wisely,
To mindfully grasp established strictures. While constraints often well serve sons
Plus daughters, during difficult occasions, offspring protest boundaries' chaffing.

"I will make it to the top! I've no disincentives, no intention to stop!
I'll extend to the big times! I'm one with purpose, soul, energy, rhyme!
Stand back world! I'm ablaze! I leap here, there, especially from home!
See my peak, my superlative point, my heightened place, incomparable!"

Convolvulaceae helps regulate temperature; their increase forms needed insulation.
Yet, per the Victorian language of flowers, such florae are a sign of "love in vain."
Witnessing a child's differentiation, no matter awkwardness, brings pride with loss.

"Suddenly, the world blurs in sunbeams' waves. Spangled ceilings coronate
Me. If I triumph, I am obliged to be the champion, the lady claiming victory.
Though, when sky high, if I collapse, expiry, too, must be recorded as mine.
Good-bye leaf. So long tree. Farewell trunk. Dearest Mommy, set me free!"

Interestingly, the seeds of many species of morning glory contain ergoline alkaloids,
LSD-like compounds. Parenting cannot ever be as altruistic as reported in the media.
No matter mothers' or daughters' relative awareness, shedding buds is less innocent.

"I sparred, hurt, fledged, advanced. My heart's thicket
Came to discern 'worldly crises' from domestic messes.
Whereas external validation rests important, I returned;
I grew up, sprouted, blossomed, wholly morning glory."

Abetted by a Need to Know

Abetted by a need to know such things, about most topics,
While lecturing on grownup sands, near swimming pools,
He failed to appreciate freshly hammered "fusion's" ken.

Thereafter, in some studies, acquired rights seemed pablum.
Standard faculties rapidly became, in literary fashion, steep
(conditions for tenure overrides, signs of eponymous folk.)

Accordingly, his brood, those would-be Ivy Leaguers,
Heads barely elevated from their books, fazed matters
Entailing aerobics, swooning at movies, lizardly lunch.

Time and success changed those brainy boobs;
Such status seekers' SERE impacted vanishing
Sororities of wives, mothers, lovers, confidents.

Consistent with cliquey perspectives, they spewed litotes,
Cached acanthus, adorned starboards with hummingbirds,
Encouraged computer meltdowns (omnificent, not fried).

Worthy diversions, more than extended weekends, finally
Culled their delvings into tossed notions, salad dressing,
Cashmere memories. Take care when studying Komodos!

Weave Dreaming

When weave dreaming, tie a pink ribbon around my big toe,
Go forward floating yellow balloons; append my headboard's rail,
Encourage fiduciary magicians to trick out doves, cards, carrots, rabbits.
Leave me smiling with Internet exchanges, moments of dire contemplation,
Maybe vellum notes scattered like so many pigeons, quadratic equations, plus
Rimmed ledges, garbage cans, tree trunks, lockers, untidy mixing bowls, and honey.

Urban peregrination, too often yields guns, roses, hot-blooded viscera.
Allegedly, blue-tongued skinks appreciate unsullied aplysia by the mouthful.
Afterwards, concision, as found in grapes grown from snouts, some telegraphs,
Diamonds develop, more often than not, in masterly evocations of artistic roving.
Given a hint of wild boar meat, most politicians are wont to take benefit from trust
Funds, balletomanes, rhinestone-studded singers, pep bands, maybe even epicene zebras.

Consider that disallowing universal patterns of curling merely brings all atoms,
Whose electronics might flop, accents leaflets falling far from favored data streams.
Likewise, real, interpersonal losses cull ill-advised twenty-somethings' waterworks,
Reduce those kids to humbleness, cause entire cities to overlook meaningful decrees.
Increased anxiety concerning vitamins' freshness dates, watering mirpesset shrubbery,
Staying possessed of plans for hot meals, fails to compensate intimately and otherwise.

Loving One's Chavrusot:
Authentic Brotherhood Evidenced at a Wedding

Hands in hands, hands on shoulders, swaying, rocking, sighing, singing, lifting
Ever light, bright, righteously invigorated, virtuous in energizing generations'
Reach, in partnership, the next best, deluxe, most excellent, unparalleled peak.

Seeking, searching, questing, the bridegroom, when not spiraling in Shamayim,
Pulls rabbis, fathers, friends, other loved ones, a dash higher, a madregah more,
Cashes in special spiritual investments while hoisting wedding guests forward.

Some near-caliente wagging of limbs brings joy beyond ken, luminosity enough
That this royal personage, this chattan flies, again, from his trumpet-filled party,
Beyond, flutes, drums, oboes, to that singular, complex station of highest virtue.

His incomparable movements spin G-d's Glory past chuppah silk, beyond kallah
Radiance, clear of celebrants' gauche, worldly finery pending supernal altitudes
Converge, beckon, set afire, loyal torches for this most enthusiastic of husbands.

Plunged back to the mundane, the tedious and regular, he again heaves the crowd
Toward shiny radiance parallel to dancing life's principle worthiness. He spreads
Good fortune, elevates an entire community, fortifies all of the holy klipspringers.

Transformed into heirs, legatees to ethereal emotions, recipients of benevolence,
Men embrace truth-spangled illumination, otherworldly chromatics, pious tones.
Together, doctors, lawyers, plumbers, roshei yeshivot, turn to ceaseless splendor.

Then the angels rebuff, puff at dutiful ears, falter keen feet, cover eyes; as if select
Semitones, those heralding ultimates, continue to be too profound for mortal flesh.
Only the kittel-decked can trespass, encroach, enter the quintessentials of Creation.

Unlike the Teenage Attitude
Attributed to the Prime Minister's Dalliances

Unlike the prime minister's dalliance, with twin Barbados maidens,
One St. Thomas guy, a bobcat, all jinked by an occasional scirocco,
Our family phone's ongoing summons to contemplate giant lizards,
Books wrought from cocobolo, also comfy devices for urging locals
To embrace commercial doohickeys, expurgate files, pilfer vintems,
Brings home all manner of card sharks, especially faro-loving guys,
Centerpieces featuring gorse, maybe adolescent sprezzatura, besides
Jack rabbit mittens, also fossicking Grand Basset Griffon Vendéens.

Most relatives strive, making meaning from empty, familial concerns,
Women's air pistol events, mixed martial arts, plus dominance located
In zebra meat. Swimming in tarns, in good 'ole summertime, ordinarily
Remains invigorating. Yet, strumming berimbaus replete with sardonic
Fleas continues strumming as a matter of taste. In handpicked caliches,
Semi-precious stones go vilely-covered. Garnets, no matter coruscating
Or not, better cryptogamic life (except where cedars, acacias, oleasters,
Cypresses petrify, yielding marketable goods). After, insouciance rules.

Swimming in Shamayim: Jacob Nissim Bensussen

Water runs downhill, toward old, unfathomable springs,
Where kedusha, emunah, origin mingle. Familial tears,
The ministrations of the chevrah kadisha, the quietness
Of tahara, and, later, of some soda among sandwiches,
When respect poured by callers is shared recollections,
Connections fashioned by dint of immersed uprightness.

No midbar here; Torah's perfumed fluids flowed
Through Yaakov to his son, daughter, wife, friends.
Life meant joy as oceans, mazel as rains. Cleansed
In teachers' precepts, in Hashem's rectitude, what
Exocrine glands confused, his neshemah streamed,
Overflowing quantities of the universe's unctures.

His smiles soaked easily, his compassion saturated
Others' dryness, steeping away pains of separation
From G-d, from klal, from self, in valued streams.
With ear, with eye, with hand, he infused b'tochen,
Unified Maker and creation. Lustrous with mitzvot,
Jacob Nissim Bensussen, zt"l, swims in Shamayim.

Savta's Bijou

Delicately worked small item,
Oddly perfect, budding moue,
Undreamed of newborn toes,
Fumaria-blossomed fingertips,
Also, delicate sparrow thighs.

As fair a dinkum as all before,
Exotic, stridulating miniature,
Tiny wonder, splendid miracle,
Boy as everyday as raindrops,
Exists as beloved "grandson."

All of the Personal Fringes of Prayer

All of the personal fringes of prayer, those whispers, murmurs, rustlings, remain
For affixing appreciation to dandelions, nettle, the rhizomes of Orchis mascula,
Besides Orchis militaris, in fighting bronchitis, maybe tuberculosis, and asthma.
Twilight's stars, at alarming moments, appear distinctly removed from heavens.

Bogged down by candies, drink, hookah pipes, street drugs, fashionistas' advice,
Many souls look aft from others' faces, suck television's teats when sitting shiva,
Neglect the wedding of humanity and G-d, the universe's exquisiteness, marvels
Typified by alley cats, kangal fish, capybaras, plus this sphere's musical insects.

Emunah, instead of some spewed patterning of memorized, clumsy components,
Continues on as more precious than any soothsayer's insights, sparkly fantasies,
Shiny things that bypass dissonance-evoking events (setting off no private glory
at the highest echelons of distrait worship). We're dumb to stuff, so reality hurts.

Added compassion, new tolerance, further dollops of imperfect courage, & wee hope,
Allow individuals to disregard some hegemonic patterns, clinch snow, rain, dewdrops,
Herald the blooming of roses, violets, wild oats, escape past faraway social strictures,
While tangoing in terebinth, lemon, plus olive groves, watered by formerly dry wadis.

51

Trenchant bells, golden light, the whisper of brief zephyrs, a donkey's bray, bleating
Sheep, too, transport tomorrow's solidarity with yesterday to focus, front and center,
Fan-stilled bodies on aspirations, to introduce home remedies to complex dilemmas.
From Jericho to the Dead Sea, humanity witnesses linnets overwintering in badlands.

Near my doorway, white agaves thrust blossoms. No aloe vera, these plants could
Feed hungry mouflon and arkars, whose pelage's remain esteemed by forthcoming
Fair, city kids, youth with vulnerabilities held hourly, "safe" or not from guerillas'
Poniards—they employ ordinary language to merit Shamayim's commissionaires.

Temporarily, residents, tourists, voyeurs, we remember the cost, in discrete lives,
Of beholding the intense dark blues, also blacks, of our celestially special sector.
Until silver shofars cry, awaiting where the satori of believers will carry susurrus,
We linger, anticipating the taking of delivery, the receiving of holy amplification.

Other Olden, "Logy" Communications

Given our present dearth of overall decent characters, those folks, who might vault beyond
Current mutagenicity, continue to advise sheltering among obdurate guardians, skipping all
Peripatetics.

Carpine minds esteem temporal and fiduciary investments of an anodyne nature, highly praise
Potemkin village rhetoric. They "esteem" preventing corsairs' infiltration, pilfering, pillaging,
Mores.

It's not dysthymia, but erstwhile abnormal functions, which appear sound, in lieu of random
Flummery, pusillanimous tribute, chin feathers, donkey tails, baldrics, hiccups, maybe asps'
Tongues.

Unlike most fireplace analogies, supports for ideas, whether sourced from cognitive spanners
Or from hammer-like habitués accustomed to hot beverages, dewars, tea service, horse sense,
Stink.

Bute, akin to fresh analgesic drugs, offers no resistance to infernal plots, yet stays
    on as popular.
(We now clinch adamantine beliefs per: Insen scale's, vinegar malts', wilding's,
    Communism's suitability.)

Moreso, choropleth maps, from which we learn "collective truths:" cull Internet
    music, use
Buprenorphine for opioid addiction, reject homeopathic dental treatments, mostly
    hang back
Laughably.

Furthermore, vellichor is yesteryear's parlous moment. Civility, too, stays
    antiquated; none
Seek tokens of proven decorum, manners explored in archives, prayers, other
    olden, "logy"
Communications.

Ultimately, pogonips, thunder storms, khamsins, equally trouble engaged cleaning
    crews;
"Ordinary," exiguous messes, whose polyphonic cores resound boldly, cause
    unrelenting
Biliousness.

Nonintimates

Sneering at Womanizing Linguistics

Womanizing language, all acrolein, frequently ablates old expressions,
Since ill-fated suborning terms, eventually go missing in social fashion.
Aggrandized self-worth's misogynous bullies assist preying monsters,
Lunch on emotional incontinence, corrugated mentations and hysteria.
Perfidious pop rhetoric, chimerae sprouted from communal estivating,
Adjust spoken intercourse's amphisbaena to cold-blooded perishables.

Such texts invent saturated sriraclta verbs, sessile nouns, greige adjectives,
Mean to create thralls out of otherwise liberated, critical thinking females.
Propose to place ladies, like matryoshka dolls, to reave, or otherwise stove,
Their machismo brio, played off of feint-warped self-image, bad hair days,
Declare, "that's not my damage" while tooting hatred of girls, also women
(proving many individuals are no more than dondering idiots, toilet tissue.)

Obstreperous chaps, unaware of ifrits of static ethics, compensate, equipoise
Their drought of corporeal chipolatas with spiteful reflections, worse words.
Sibilant orators, certain disempowered dilatants, avoid important gatherings
Desideratum sharpens their linguistic advantage, cyberspace waggles them.
Notice, divisive critters, made by press releases, sup athwart, not vertically.
They lubricate, normally, via copious amounts of Champaign plus fentanyl.

Funny, such authorities on parkour get invited out or in. Scarce limitations
Form automatically near screed. Girlfriend and her sister are hardly stupid.
All things considered, suasory depredation carries on no higher or uplifted
Than gum wads, mangles, dead hedgehogs, termites, or ball peen hammers.
Political churls, men who prevaricate when confronted, hang around as less
Useful than sheep nadgers, sporks, tree spinach, & consanguineous cousins.

Voguing with Current Federal Bureaucrats

It avails science writers to try to promote military splendor.
Sucking funding from objectionable parties phases mundanities.
These days, it's voguing with current federal bureaucrats that brings riches.

In contrast, camping in theatres' utility rooms attracts cockroaches,
Triggers bits of plaster to fuel demands for therapists, thaws out idiots
Intent on taking over urban bodegas or on spilling users' viscera in parks.

The worst penury's smoothly synthesized by those suit and sunglasses types,
Who yield when declaring all manners of balderdash, slinking toward shadowy
Testimonies, spurred by the likes of cartoon characters, cheap wine, stale cookies.

To sate more than cutpurses, it's necessary to addend stilted footnotes,
Practice tantra yoga, open one's palms to starbursts, guzzle bad radiation.
(Synthesized electricity's a tricky matter that perhaps won't act predictably.)

Leaning on utility tables, writing copious records about army experiences,
Promises only to unpack paradigms, not to drive away moggies, rats, ravens.
Declining opportunities to leave districts unprotected evokes worse neighbors.

Electing, instead, to smooth incommensurate barbs could bring peace,
Lower tax rates, cause an increase in births around holiday times. Also,
Trading spectacles beholdens traitors to piecework, gym workouts, vitamins.

When I grow up, I'll set sail around corporate illusions, hire pals, eat taffy.
Otherwise, I'll plan days so that martial innovations can readily destroy cities,
After rolling over foreign forces unwilling to pay tributes in gold or fine textiles.

Compliance in settling desert development towns equals insanity, excluding
When payola fountains over various companies' courtiers, dance halls, clinics.
As such, social drives succeed in raising more than the cost of biscuits or sunshades.

Matters of Mens Rea

The enhancement of the Magna Carte,
Impacted, evidentially, Ivy League dorms,
Raised the specter of fascinating themes,
Including sedition's principal witnesses.

History reports deciding international conflict,
Got noticed by means of Gutenberg projects,
As directed by flechettes, kite wires, daggers,
Possibly also glabrous and heavy cross bows.

Within the bedchamber of critical thinkers,
Naked leaders are still unwilling to spend,
At all costume jewelry or literary devices,
On cherished others or on virtual strangers.

In the end, when nibbling local fauna, some viverridae
Insist ferrying humans to amusement centers' cousins,
Cinemas, bowling alleys, concert venues, and the UN,
Causes incomplete governments to wheeze cud, abort.

During Allegorical Surveys

Dusting allegorical surveys in five directions of plastered fancy and hiccupping philters,
Blathering imperfect truths, forgoing telepathic recall, failing to catch morning's refrain,
All bring about the genus of sentiments that can be beneficial fertilizing bovine pastures.

Uprooting palpable health, entirely, means: running aground in sailboats of foundlings,
Pulling closer to enigmas (whose sinusoidal characteristics present as green and rotten),
Equally, catalyzing the extension of bribes to local newspapers and random furze-pigs.

One zone's adversary can become the next ones's best buddy under dazzling conditions;
No écrivaine lodged in a boat's fo'c'sle, or fashioned, with pitch, against acme elements,
Regardless of verb types, otherwise helps /guides populations towards abandoning lidos.

The French notion of mise en place barely addresses the requisites of moorhens, javelinas,
Etheric beings; searching for foreign beauty aids makes for puns, not topological solutions.
Music undergirded by a lack of moral principles, likewise, can't be executed on berimbaus.

Right Lights of a Copy Machine

Red lights of a copy machine, candles, elevator boxes, cliffs near the ocean,
High school lore, that which sings of gaily trudging toward aromatic plants,
Many years imprisoned on knolls near seafloors forgoing phosphorescence,
While folks provide craggy stories, rebuffed merit, brandymel, steel-cut oats.
Nepotism in the Old World, protexia in the new, underpaid heroines pursue,
Hence, to integrate unkind mentations into children's conception of "teens."

'pity we elect to arrange growing up with trilled, doubled jealousy, not truth,
To equip generations with religious items, craft, not farming, tools, not words.
Veracities only suck away courage if creature discourse enhances cowardice.
Muse over poisonous, emotional quinzhees leaving precious saplings fragile,
Plaintive, melancholic chants discount values, except profitable MP4 copies,
Desktop microphone broadcasts, present YouTube wonders, aunties' purses.

Thursday nights, lots of souls search spaces for ethically meager, imagined roots,
Spill developmental crawling, dire notices, moral visions, uncomfortable images,
In local dressing rooms, within nursing homes, throughout taverns, airports, jails.
Without strength for stressing socially relevant cognates, "running away" results
In troubles: growing older, trusting cab drivers not to exploit the system, perhaps
Bites of fermented tobacco sucked down alongside of artificially formed shakes.

When magnificent red and gold hues, most frequently associated with billboards,
Arrive at whatever constitutes a new gobsmack, inhabitants numbering hundreds
Scatter dears, aliens, four color prints, or seasonal delights in the queen's private
Bathroom. Daily doses of manga cure no ills, but affix motility to physical ethics,
Especially when instigating actions of individuals prolix with complaints, distrait
Noises, read aloud out-of-the box outlooks, grievous cheese, negligible reactions.

Underrated as a Crummy Texts

Benign neglect remains far too satisfying
As introduction to announcing bathroom
Intentions for most reporters to abandon
Accounts of relative progress & function
Oblivious to others.

Additional convergent media flatter no one
Beyond satellite dishes, ailurophiles, ricers,
Cause nouns, intent upon partying on snow
Days, presidents' birthdays, few weekends,
To rooted in junky predictions.

Dingles, dunderdoodles, fluffheads, odd balls,
All ought never to be vended underestimated;
Idiots exist among barkeeps, nurses, politicians.
Metallic-colored cars stink like soured tzatziki,
Deprived of personal growth.

Tracking home pages' cough syrup ads,
Reading users' histories, jumping trains,
Engaging in algebra, deflecting torture,
Proves unhealthy unless mutual efforts,
Return for s'mores.

Vacations, more than aggregates of shopping,
Cartoons, or amusement parks, evoke pirated
Victories, lost tickets, trinkets, shabby things,
Transmute consumer examples on parenting,
Support insanity.

Immediately, the amount/kind of individual utility
Depends on equating electronic education with fun.
Suspiciously, a head space's price of breath remains
Following bungee jumping, maybe re-embodiment.
(See enclosed.)

Characters and Old Crocked Pots

Wonky characters, old crocked pots,
Such international breeders, at bus stops,
Willingly add work to hummingbird rosters.

Cosmic singularities sleep, at least,
Over van tops of midlife matrons pieced
Together under careful eyes of select thieves.

Domestic divas, don't ya know,
Use stepstools when they come/go,
Employ themselves at poodle shows

When we're driven to organize
Good and welfares, all supersized,
It's best for bright beasts to synchronize.

Child-friendly publications
Among mass media's virile stations,
Trump most private, preschool educations.

Scouts build places cleaner, better paths,
Construct shiny bridges, which tend to last
Allow no others' assembled succors to surpass.

Lumbago, or, minimally, acute pain,
Viewed through contemporary medicine,
Boils down, repeatedly, to experts' negligence.

The Basis for Evil Machinations

It's currently clear that the basis for evil machinations provides
For rabidly dissecting decaying crawfish, also select mustelids.

When delivering copious sets of notes regarding archaic formulas,
Pride plus joy in chemical engineering, children's drugged faces,
Rhetoric gets focused not on clouds, but on irresponsible choices.

Toying with flypaper's coating can trigger stable angels to sidle
Beyond external interferences, sclera, cornea of goats' eyeballs,
Actions implemented to benefit, plumbago blossoms, energetic
Liana, all manner of cosmic retribution, and caches of grendilla.

Coteries of customers, constituted by self-combusting halfwits,
Regularly retain ample vigor to emancipate from ministrations
Related to activities engaging fashions with business machines,
Raising the specter of overcooked rice, wrongly donned profits,
Even popular draughts, since major intricacies are smoke-filled.

Enduring frightening failure enables publics to recognize dupes,
To extract money from indulged reptiles, high Cs from musettes,
Farts from doormen (global peace's big deterrent isn't politics.)
Rather, we ought to electronically post: offers for cheap houses,
Internet addresses of skilled luthiers, six ways to soup old peas,
Plus share data on second-tier Olympian repechages' locations.

More burnt than unrequited industrial growth, love rejected makes
Selling bodies wholesale, a mottled, itchy, sadistic process. Laugh.
Bits and pieces of sinew, fat, not unlike honeyed ethanol, refortify
Sordid, steel-plated apertures when vogueish monsters go missing.
Infusoria are naught, relative to the menacing erosion activated by
Offshore wages, externalized anxieties, "therapeutic alternatives."
Publicized altruisms continue anyway, all low calorie and useless.

As high hillocks of clothing, discarded by few eclectic investors,
Observed doing tedious exercises in animal husbandry, gratifies.
Kings wisely expect that abandoning all local pound's denizens,
And supping roadkill, pleasing social dragons with dead syntax,
Yields grand pouches of kinfolks sufficiently distressed to assay
Clandestine engagements linking darling epicene critters. Added
Ingested substances, thereafter, get commoners' vats of seldom
Verified belief, issued without validations, scruples & blessings.

In balance, usually, indigenous hockey, lacrosse, free tag, basketball players,
Bereft of protective gear, in legal courtyards, high school fields, newsstands,
Brutalize regular human understanding out of themselves, out of each other.
Their interactions (little more than lame declarations, heavy makeup, flash),
Not ever allow the stymieing of opinions brought down by educated classes.
Despite myriad proposals to the contrary, such negotiations get repurposed,
Outwardly directed, or just referenced in the midst of media costermongers.
Hoodwinking the populace, permanently transforming sanguine inhabitants
Into Komodo dragon food rots regardless of the frequency of feeding times.

Pigeons in Oakland

Pigeons in Oakland,
Picking at peanuts,
Ignore straw-hatted
Students learning guitar
To support chemical habits.

One sole banjo player, who
Donned florescent orange,
As well as a blue macaw,
Challenges the sky,
Dares the dark clouds.

Elsewhere, lightning
Strikes here and again.
A sandaled gypsy girl,
Rimmed in shadow,
Rhinestones, pathos,
Loosens a buckle.

Or By Inland Lakes

There's no coin proffered in media circuses or by inland lakes. Reinventing
Polemic selves makes for the deconstruction of disposable determinations.
Professionals routing against wickedness, pilfered by seagoing comedians,
Consume more sheep than men "smart enough" to face perfidious hunters.

We'd not bother to care, ever again, to face down lemans if not for the sanctity
Music affords (lasting goodness wafts when speaking then grasping wisdoms.)
"Out there" live grownups that encourage the provision of colleagues' reports;
Mainly, stars offer dusky backdrops for an appreciation of rudimentary verity.

Answers formed by moonbeams or casual light reflected off of rounding bellies,
Old wiley enemies, their eyes larger than dinner plates, their knives unsheathed,
Charge that gestation, childbirth, and nursing transfer undeserved wonderment.
Population swells, potency in women, also in panegyrics, corroborate cognates.

In a generation or so, maybe youngsters, seamed to their life mission, will serve,
Strong, thick trunks, made large despite prematurely felling, writing about mud.
Connections webbing from Skokie to Hebron, express healing because of faith.
Boy phenoms guard vows posed by ugly dogs growling technology; pain hurts.

Corporate Life in a Goldfish Bowl

"Life's," a simple word, four letters, more complex than
Longer wonders; "conflate," "promote," and "purchase,"
Disguises possibilities working beyond commercial tang,
Instinctive to raw unfurling of multiple periods' sagacity,
Activated by conversations in which others can't engage.

Dear cohorts forward generous, eschatological sentiments,
When gold or brown cloth treasures, bookcases' brimming
With varicolored sleeping bags, fabric backpacks, attitude,
Sidle unorthodoxly (following wooden signs) along fences,
Jockey silken threads, or foxtrot among wretched car boots.

Secrets despise boundaries, run radically albedo whilst shushed,
Seek out billboards, megaphones, access to SEO search engines,
Inner city graffiti, slingshot telemarketing, sundry pretty ponies,
'til dry cleaning solvent, white vinegar, and borax are employed
To remove the dust, sweat, dung of extra prized grandiloquence.

Supervisors eventually remain alert late enough to return votes,
Recalling how their managerial reactions, all egregious choices,
Plus their colleagues' belief that peers seem capable of bunkum
(children act childish), gets compromised as publicized records
Concerned with juxtaposing chaste referents and urbane jetsam.

Important institutions and individuals yield negligible estimations,
Of sociopsychology resulting in maladroit communication events.
Symbolic, linguistic, aretaic, additionally normative conceptions,
Nonmaterial cultural elements, remain of consequence to writing.
(Boardroom assessments yet provide silage to the unempowered.)

Reluctant to Use Their Words

Modern heroes, and their familiars, operate reluctant
To use their words for relaying public opinion spins,
Suffered in private circles, closets, or official caches.
For it seems low-context societies' leaders publicize
Popular sentiment through broad, designer curricula.

Folks from morbid waitstaff, in regal dining halls,
To woodland byways' tenants, toady, no exposed
Parental underwear, charity, or pantoums, depend
On perceived truth, lack of justice, warrior faults.
High tech, agricultural, or military potency reign.

Holiness, more than other recently received real estate
Beyond clipped meadows, luminescent paper goblets,
Multiple cigarette butts, Grandpa's sort-sleeved shirts,
Proffers better deep sales fish than do corporate jocks.
Wirelesses, test kitchen results, turgid voters indicate.

Past midlife, ranking surpasses media-sodden affrays.
Not constantly, just sometimes, supports underdogs,
Promotes marriage businesses, portrays relationships
As not once amounting to cocooning, cooing, calling,
Not for cultural intent, long periods, fame, and profit.

Puppy Dogs and Feral Cats: An Urban Beddy-Bye

Puppy dogs, some feral cats, also monkeys screeching brightly,
Make happen bird-like junk that's blue, mucousy, so sightly.

Such that parklets' go-rounds of curls, of silly children chanting,
Cause giggly chasing thru the rain, lets guns replace old ranting.

Hurt stinks, once roosting high amongst friends on mimsy hills,
When nascent, uncertain goings-on dispute the common will.

Lambie footfalls construct games, solely as rivalry of friends,
As chipmunks, anacondas, skinks, slink by best caged ends.

Thereafter, confident vegans move to Middle Eastern climes,
Volunteer for urban work, mess with provincial hills, vines.

Black radishes, like sea green ferns, mallards displaying proudly,
What's more, forms of lagniappe, repair denizens rather stoutly.

Tiny cherries, icicles, last season's clover blossoms, too,
Makes great work of private cops, of eating fresh fugu.

Seems retarded that those short, fat crowding subway jocks,
Remain ignorant of city stink, although wear yuppie socks.

It could be that doctors, carpenters, journeymen of kinds,
Fixated with the Sophists' works, besides orange rinds,
Might be able to halt this nonsense (I surely doubt it.)

Given that all pit bulls, software hacks, diffuse gurus via glare,
The rest of us low-context folks stay too hurt to chiefly care.

Personal, unified breaks, wrought from standing on some ledges,
Return us to urban pets, to regular roustabouts' fresh pledges.

Of That Particular Ilk

Anxiety-strung or not, packrats,
Forbearers, of that particular ilk,
Ran from exposure of straddling
Views hardened by coarseness.

Else wonderful friends, those tools,
Enamored with political rhetoric,
Objectified fiduciary well-being,
Plus Amazon.com's pet notions.

Certainly that sailboat of himself, cartwheeled
Along his tongue, his clothing frayed to fibers.
(Sushi, avocado-sourced, needs polished rice,
maybe, circulating money, and a lead in races.)

During a break while she dallied, assigned other
Patients, stopped fleeing, scrutinized participants,
She kept on spawning words, ideas, also pigeons,
She began investing in anacondas, escaped artists.

Doctor to pharmacist, the couple claimed dual
Relationships seemed better than rash weight.
They'd no appreciation for hotel lobbies, mad
Bovine pens, park bathrooms, public gardens.

In the guise of odd codfish, sweet, special spheres,
Their allocation of ambuyat dishes proceeded 'til
Government employees, maybe lawyers, ceased
Attacking from fresh angles or sending marmots.

Other followers, in turn, trying coercions of sorts,
Sounding off. Never again, that girl allowed love,
For things pertaining to "character development,"
Any heights she breathed, or consecrated domains.

The Mage's Incomplete Solace

I purr to myself; no one else works clever enough to wrestle silver-fanged beasts,
Alone, during shore walks, combining brine from disparate lands' asylums.

I sing to myself; no one else demonstrates successfully built connections,
Among tawny dandelion, green-leafed sorcery, acerbic enchantments.

I talk to myself; no one else listens with equal terse, attentive charm,
While disassembling possible futures, thistle-like energy, scurvy.

I keep to myself; no one else imparts my predisposition toward lice,
Amidst psychic awareness, astute probing of hinterland buoyancy.

I worry myself; no one else's consolations stream from capitulums' sacred cavities,
When strumming perdition for founding citadels, or championing unredeemables.

I shock myself, no one else's behest brings branded sheep, studied knots,
Among parasomatic links, as well as redirected water and indiscretions.

I deride myself; no other dallying causes thermodynamic angst, ionic rage,
During: transforming from maid to crone, morphing from tatters to rags.

I despise myself; no one else's archetype squeezes personal valor, old mischief
Since rising suns, wild daisies, winging geese, young sentries, spiders shiver.

Whispers of Wilderness

Municipal libraries, moon-faced lovers,
Large portions of most general publics,
Especially persons with pocket money,
Booked seats at tonight's cosmic vista.

They grasped that silo-preserved grain,
Revealed photographs of bait pooches,
Plus minute measures of wild carrots,
Supported naive disdain of road safety.

As such, composition texts, stolid rhetoric,
Convey compassion capable of conveying
Simurgh wings, bakery-made mignardises,
Icy liminal young morphing like raindrops.

Romantic and occupational relationships,
Shelf fungi pounded into chowder dust,
Repairmen secured against winter wind,
Ostensibly aid farces residing forthwith.

While clean-diapered, pint-sized children,
Participate in expensive, exhausting drills,
(exercises meant to waste public sources),
Precious fingers tug all ensuing miracles.

Possibly, babies, stallions' divots, also,
As well as cameras, computers, tanpuras,
The sort of entertainment that's costly,
Whisper wilderness near hills' havens.

Whether Equine or Strigine

Whether equine, or strigine, whether of skies or grand pastures, mostly, visitors to virtue
Will come away with more than brilliant pictures; they: laugh a loud in places where one
Might, ordinarily: hold shy, hiccup (until rolling over in mirth), regard "secrets" as though
No one else is bounded, show facial glee for plastic bags of milk, ignore zebra crossings,
Disregard lizards seeking asylum in kitchen cabinets (when forced to survive housecats.)

Whereas small, European and North American presses are loath to sign Middle Eastern
Authors, tropological words mean so much to the majority of global denizens. After all,
In the New World, when regarding almonds' fuzzy green outer peel, negotiating socks,
Encouraging a doctor to write an unnecessary script, low-context, verbal-oriented motes
Remain the norm as brumbies seek lives free of putrescence no matter relative charges.

Before children fledge, vacationers pack toothbrushes in their carry-ons, but leave back
Their Waterpiks, as well as their magical memories of holy places viewed through lens.
Just as taste in art varies, equally do "reasons" for ethnic conflict. Some allude intellects
Produce and distribute "rhetorical messes." Others aver that an international willingness
To experience, but not to notice, how ecolinguists' ideas conveys poor peace prospects.

Even when not meaning to boost mouths' corners, certain gaffes become the equivalent
Of smarmy grins, blurring the beauty otherwise beheld by generations-old compassion.
(Recipes for hummus are insufficient souvenirs for travels marking outings among good
Men.) Rather, transforming through revising claims phonier that cubic zirconium could,
Perchance, stir the planet; our tribute to monotheistic fidelity is more than long overdue.

Covered with a Leotard

An enormous, local lady,
With a red, oozing pimple,
In the middle of her face,
Squeezed one more tomato.
Her brown hands clutched,
Thereafter, burst that fruit,
Onto her print dress, maybe.

Adjacent, a rain-soaked cat,
Walking curves of muscle,
Visible beneath spotted skin
Covered with a leotard.
Eyes wide, sentient, peered,
Surveying all the city shuk,
Observed pried fruit, maybe.

Later, a gang of children,
Singing, stealing, skipping
Punctuation, good grammar,
Manners, pinched the lady.
And crowded the cat, while
Merrily stuffing bon mots
Into coat pockets, maybe.

When Adopting Great Dangers

When adopting great dangers, from the moment media crews feel surprised,
Ostensibly for purposes of health, episodes occur whenever horse whisperer
Viscera, like pipas, get sacrificed for bugles, for the costs of scrub teams—
Court fees, emotional damages burgeon. Western sensibilities, forfeit local
Heritage, money, fame. Seats by lookers remain cheerfully sanguine jokes.

The ordinary, passive, to the point of inertness, rudiments, at few parallels,
Create delightful slapstick like art culled from moldy cheese, horse manure,
A lifetime's worth of thrown way school salary, windfall aimed at paupers.
Potpourri cats' sensibilities notwithstanding, truckloads of craggy loyalists
Seem likely to hand over yerba santa for all matters of respiratory disorders.

It's also true that balancing recent sons-in-law, science degrees, thespians,
Technical staff, movers, maybe turns in the local soup kitchen, taxes, plus
Scattered tongue-in-cheek references, countermands significant searches.
Flute lessons for six, bowling lanes admission coupons, and chaya quiche
Ain't cheap, were never meant to grouch, sing, cry, extol expiration dates.

It endures as confounding that returning again to crime scenes, cleaners
Tracks emotional, psychological, also symbolic mud. None prize assets
Beyond litigious borders. Sixty thousand bright orange goldfish, groats,
Taciturn self-definitions, relationships, social status, bucket lists smirk;
Monstrous cultivars, i.e. amphora lanky enough for snuggling, don't fit.

75

Thereafter, missing portions of dosh, designated for emergent missiles,
Highway meridians' beneficial weeds, strange statements, anatomically
Correct East Village marzipan, showing Catalina Islands' ferry chiefs,
Waxed mustaches, weepy kinds, as well as glass-eyed oncologists, gift
"In kind" to zombies trussed in afterglow thoughts, pinchers, escargots.

Travel, real estate, sundry former purchases, serve best gently heated
Over empirical sensibilities or collective law suits. Kissy girls shrill.
Moral lessons, covered in thick stratums of family-oriented gambols,
Man-eating pythons, love, loss, and the illicit use of select ceramics
Keep rocking peanut butter/jelly sushi, Furry conventions, intellects.

A million dollars, blended by a simple barkeep, accompanying just a
Penthouse. Retired MIT researchers, rodents, satchel painters, chaste
Beatniks, careening taxicab drivers, ply executives' strange incidents,
Purple buds, amidst building conflicts, delivered in individual bowls.
(What's truly essential swallows sponsors, deludes Junior Leaguers.)

The Sanctity of Lists

Incidental characters, after all, amongst poor choices,
Continue commemorating lifetimes of joint to joven.
Their mouthfuls situate twix drams, puffs, & fey dust,
Strings of pearls, bijoux, ceramic dribs as balderdash.

The sanctity of lists, declared in infinite teenage wisdom,
When prudent ones assimilated, or, on account of human
Complexity or growth, raised dead from charnel houses,
Weighed fibbing vs. chocolates, lauded crying nonsense.

Most haver evolves; it's supposed, to ward off bankruptcy.
Partnerships between disenfranchised fish, neglected birds,
Bear witness to such refuse as to judder the most grounded
Peristaltic movements back to soliloquies spun during war.

If ever transversing an eigenstate, escort all palaver past the dockets.
Proceedings in lawsuits concerning low brows strafing flight lanes,
Collecting murder weapons, valuing orpiment, bring about the total
Loss of personal rehabilitation, a creation of more Russian Mafiosi.

Clerical canticles, matins, couplets, similarly inharmonic, crave power
Enough to offset racial hatred, domestic abuse. Gawping alike babies.
Few ancient settlers closed themselves, rejected gilded virtues, morph
Contentious within the confines of their spans' ordinary ramifications.

In doubting the veracity of troublesome reports, or light, loose trousers,
Insisting on playing camera obscura media games, folks, on the whole,
Guys were running to medically assist terrorist bus bombings' victims,
Daily rekindled zeal while making websites' worth of jaded comments.

Common, unremitting testimonies recall to mind, given the doctor-gardeners,
Esca, whales, parrots, corvids grieve at runaway moments of loving kindness.
No plinth can possible support the hate of denizens mouthing rural platitudes.
Dingers reflecting on tawdry, unsung networks of siblings, or corrupt cousins.

Seltzer and Other Social Signifiers

Urbane bubbles, sure translucent giddiness parceled for kiddies.
Adults like better, we're told, sparkling wine, fermented twice,
Nicely wrapped in ribboned bottles, pricey, that wet kings' sip,
Unlike Borscht Belt gas, comically-rated for Hebraic families.

Each Elderly Face

After many ill-managed attempts to divest from techy friends,
I grasped a bouquet of elderly faces. Those exquisite psychic
Vessels possessed lifetimes' worth of articulated meditations,
Joys, regrets. Visage gifts, opened, more than festooned large
Worshipper numbers chanting back select wrongdoings, hope.

Half my baby doll's dress, plus a florican photo (all ruffled study),
Carted two hundred leagues food and fashion treasures, specified
Women's roles in fairly indistinct sentences gaged by loucheness.
Garbage duty, scrubbing patios with a toothbrush, giving parkour
Competitors, other mud-caked kids, outsourced sensibilities, rots.

Large print nonverbals are needed; oldsters share. Grown kids, too, require
Field stations for Martian experiments, skipping stones, bundled donations.
When seniors morph into misshaped manikins or quivering kludge, we lose.
It remains far better to amass girlfriends, honor menses, births, menopause,
While ignoring Facebook, Instagram, Twitter, WeChat, and QZone ratings.

Seeking youth disreputably becomes discarding diadems, saxophones, lessons.
Braying thru convergent channels, painting cedars, acacias, myrtle, & cypress,
Humping off advice given some celestial "rank," in the end, brings stagiaires,
The worst sort. In time babies toddle home, seek parents' sagacious stymieing.
The leaf falling freely tears less than the one insistent upon adhering to a twig.

Truth As Informed by Art and Architecture

Given our clinging to vast social liabilities, our agonizing over eclectic
Academic work, like semiotics, structural products of fresh mentations,
Like dialoging with readers, adding & subtracting stability components,
Transcriptions, thus, become reasonable databases for various messages
Laden in mosiaculture, soaked in ammonia, strewn along actors, events,
Modalizations provoking purpose as part of innovation's kaleidoscope.

See, "poetics" of place requires signs. "Behaviors" plus "settings" don't
Necessarily implement interdependently, nor accommodate many ethnic
Elucidations, symbolic influence on communications, or understandings.
(Definitions will sprout akin to kale from daunting, interior landscapes.)
Transcendental continua, disparate generative grammars, nurture mainly
Visual and verbal texts' juxtapositions, grow tensions vis-à-vis meaning.

On balance, possessing euphoric or disjuncted objects produce intervals
In epistemic watersheds. Linguistic convexity places personal morality
Beyond social perfection, causes relics to spin culturally relative words.
That same advantage won't get claimed by clam diggers or bullfighters;
Only select narratives are encouraged to reach status highs, to be gilded.
Ultimately, garbage men, chamber maids, urologists instill our purpose.

Granted, journalists, additional cold fish, bullfrogs, also critique prose,
Treat "truths" as important marginal proofs, laugh at central paradigms.
Likewise, chow down on bad sushi, bruit mythoi, sheltered hay stacks.
Language lacks all manner of habeas corpus also shared architecture's
Derived; prompts ontological insights. It disperses, to grand audiences,
Existential categories meant to establish "official" gatekeepers' appeal.

.

So Aloes Grew in Vietnam

I was five when bell bottom blues filled the airwaves.
Yesteryear, conscription was the etiquette fought by youth.
"Levy" was attributed to jeans, not tribes, excises or militias.
Raconteurs sang of Canada via self-mutilation, furthermore, free love.

Sanky-pankies got booked to distract suits from badminton;
Pentagon types bettered domestic rent boys in pulling out shirttails.
Together, they viewed movies, chowed through kibble, smoked weed;
Anything to circumvent ordering multitudes to jungles' killing floors.

Asking employers to equivocate, spin like monkeys,
Rank outfits as per levels of starch, payola, kickbacks,
Meant allowances for pulp stationed anywhere, but was more
Well-liked than were talking heads tergiversated boardrooms' duvets.

So aloes grew, where once some selection of mute acquaintances
Wiggled tentacles across dimity covers, stopping to pick lint, also nits.
Such bedtime vitriol got replaced often, but never because of political bribes.
Then, cypress, oleaster, also acacias, transformed into lintels, matchsticks, lamps.

Epigones, erstwhile, sorted birthday greetings, air kisses, enticements,
Refused to contend with arbitrary matchmaking of careers as well as combat
Adventures. Pressing answering machines, apprising salaries, pinching clerks
Helped corporate hicks, mayhap, with silver-plated luncheons, lapel pins, stogies.

Local ethnics, blared melodiesy sufficient to erase bosses' celebrations,
Those quondam lieutenants, less-than-kickshaw in dungarees, meanwhile,
Practiced no-nonsense ethics along with childbirth options. Clinics flourished.
If we blinked adequately, clicked our heels, inverted our eyes, they fluttered away.

KJ Hannah Greenberg

A Flash Mob for Holiday Shoppers

At arm's length, beyond, snowflake girls, total Senior Skip Day,
Whirl to electronic music, shopping tempos, the shrill of friends.
Ear buds pop like summer daisies, metal, rock, classic tweet out.

Old Man Hortance claps, stomps, whistles a bit.
Local theatre brings teens with antlers winking,
Shimmying, shaking tails, tuning cheeks to red.

Turning tricks near neighborhood totems, instead
Of pirouetting higher on stage, triggers yearning;
Suddenly, there's a need to curtsy the food court.

Tall pulls of soda later, six of them jaunt on elbows,
Break spectacles, loose ties, scrape parts here, there.
Ariel moments cost bruises, cuts, complexion, face.

Juniper, all tulle plus sequins, pink sprigs of fleece,
Barbie-doll makeup, tinsel crown, tinfoil nose ring,
Embraces Stacy. One hundred BFFs encircle them.

Mrs. Elderidgen, hearing aid partly dislodged, shrugs.
She's busy choo-chooing hotdog into Annie's mouth.
Seeing dancers, her granddaughter misses, splits skin.

Pointing toward a glazed roast, honeyed chicken, fries,
Today's sushi special, yesterday's reduce-priced buns,
More than ninety would-be Rockettes spin, kick, caper.

At one table, salt and pepper bop nearby sugar, soy sauce,
Displacing napkins, shaking tradition, spilling, bumping
Alongside of staid utensils, used vessels, drained patrons.

Abruptly, elves, essentially yearbook plus society boys, scamper,
Such overeager marmots, prairie dogs, woodchucks, chipmunks,
Stop sampling foot longs, chop suey, long enough to gyrate a bit.

Nature and Her Children

Starlight

Far luminaries.
Outlying gas giants.
Light local trails.

First Showing

With rain, the earth blushed clematis, plus poppy.
Almond blossoms bloomed as misplaced water ice.
Veils of drought pulled back, revealed new growth.
Deep springs trembled. Wadis filled. Streams ran.
Summer skies, after, burned that vital landscape.

Patched green, then brown, the local fabric faded.
Shiravs or harmatttans tugged its verdant threads.
Time dust-coated leaves, buds, and our memories.

September

Summer's quick twilight.
Faintly trumpets fall's phases,
Changes public pallets.

Downpour

Heavy clouds BURST open!
Motorcades of happiness
Fall earthward; good crops.

Levels of Citrus

Although we've been asked for bedizened scripts, for fanciful archetypes of insouciant
Behaviors, our avidity brings about lugubrious outcomes. Consider waterfowls' modes.
Birds aren't curious about sex, don't ponder, every fortnight or so, whether possessing
Strong self-esteem makes them attractive to others; they just get started on procreation.

Despite formal rhetoric, few features are stochastic; much less is determined on a whim.
Noticeably, pandits, university deans ask proof of fabrications' positive bearing on folks.
Cultural dimensions, largely, get negotiated. Antediluvian deeds get weighed, measured.
Word slingers provide limited grasps of superannuated engines, feathery repasts, details.

Inversely, two-legged genera use urbane, enchanted pipes, legerdemain. Humans cover
Proximate magic, anathematic mechanisms, the broadcasting of aphorisms, conscience.
They make small investments in horsey rides, pictures of family, trailing small children.
(Swans and geese can't change diapers, assemble puppets for descendants, yet do care.)

See, levels of establishment's citrus byways, guarded by keepers of prestigious publics,
Deconstruct conduct per ancient code—few quiddities post more than "old provender."
Ducks' cousins, correspondingly, never worry over elements of costumes; their plumy
Suits are function, not fashion. Their generations scarcely feign more than mating calls.

Among ponds and lakes, no legacy's as precious as a good name (or panoply of bribes.
Notwithstanding vehicular sounds, which interrupt their courting rites, they're content.
Linguistic ductility, after all, unlike wilder sorts of goings-on brings sere connectivity.
Verbal palisades, all things considered, especially crossgender communications, rots.)

The Real Thing

Ethereal quiet, like mendicant urchins best upturned
hands,
Is insistence and temerity optioned out of fertility gone
awry.

In uncovering the actual status of four leaf clovers, horse shoe
crabs, websites,
Imitation titanium, alike the chances of spilling off of a roller
coaster, befuddles.
It's possible to learn, despite ads' intentions, that small children
aren't self-propelled.

Verily, wish-a-by stars, rainbows, fairy dust (when experiential
circuits blow),
Require friendships, marriage, good employment, also vodka,
to buoy passengers.
Otherwise, we abnegate; youth's no "ever after," early findings
aren't even semi-permanent.
Adolescence's redolent of semantic battlements, ballistic wordplay,
conveys interpersonal strife.

Best to pick our toes, thumb "safe" highways, warble while warding
frostbite, snore.
Generally, substitutions for authenticity suit most modern microscopes.
Plodding hamster wheels
Beat finding proxies for ill kin, crocheting apposite garments,
swimming backstroke.
During lulls, the daring adjure, while lesser folks link to untested
icebergs as well as lions' dens
(Despite the media's silenced tocsin, mainly, people manage just fine
sitting along reality's margins.)

Acquiring Provisions for Pets and Plants

Acquiring provisions for pets and plants designates,
Immediately bothering to stop impressing visiting royalty.

Mistaking "insufficient" for "necessary" grows troubles,
Routes campuses where street bums' podiums fail wallabies.

Conditional thinking drives forward weird conversations,
Means brain chow gets stuffed into fashionable, dismal writing.

Additionally, the folks embodying feminine briefcase traits;
Stockings, fishing lines, rotten mascara, continue halting armies.

This contemporary period of literature buttresses would-bes,
Amply applies herbal poultices to large weevils seeking ignominy.

Principally, history teachers bring to mind "now" trumps "before,"
Whenever banels of woolies try to substitute for moving assemblies.

Her Samurai Sheep's Revenge

Little Bo Peep bought Samurai sheep,
Since weasels eat mutton while hiding.
Thus, lads who'd unsheathe their swords,
To appropriate her and her world, were
Murdered by fleece fierce with biting.

Ah, the Aardvark: Classifying Chaos in an Urban Zoo

Ah, the aardvark, by that badger, cons a capuchin.
Then, he pauses, driving home poor dingo's wager,
Makes the elephant, egret, ermine, eel, also emu,
Fiddle alongside falcons, gannets, likewise, gnus.

Hornets' hijinx, hackees' hallucinations, as well as ibexes' notions,
Irk impalas, especially when such acts cause irascible commotions.
It's acknowledged, too, that jackdaws, jerboas, jack rabbits, jellies,
Unabashedly peruse "kissing" gouramis scooting along on bellies.

Elsewhere, lampreys laugh as loggerheads slink,
Beyond magpies, mudpups, muskrats, mink.
Plus, needlefish, nagas, nutcrackers, all get busy scrutinizing slimy newts,
Which scold shy octopi, fast osprey, maybe otters decked in fastidious suits.

Paccas perch near puffins, pandas, panthers, pups, pudus,
Quail croon along with quaggas as well as quokka cats, too,
Whenever rabbits, reindeer, sprinkboks (but not shrews),
Push tamarins, tapirs, quite all sorts of tayras; they choose.

Uakaris screech their tessitura. Voles hide in form.
Wallabys whistle to wattlebirds, woodcocks, worms.
Xyloryctes beetles march in parade, unrestrained,
Beyond yellowhammers, yapoks, ynambus so tame.

Zebu, sweat slick, run from zorilles, given visitors' little
Litter, rather than human potions, lotions, pills, or vittles,
Impart sufficient cordons hostile to hidden social skunks,
In particular, after brazen city kids present alphabet funk.

A Vicious Cycle Partially Fostered by Conks and Other Planar Groupings

Conks and other planar groupings,
Grow up suckling, rending coarse
Debris from flora-type relations.
Pores, spores, sundry bits of broken
Fiber, feeding filaments in concert.
Strange, yet absolutely staid, strands slough
For truffle hunters, folks seeking forest food.

Rangers, furthest remote persons, relay
Surveys, knots, first-aid, compasses, and scat,
Fire-starting, cloth-style signaling, maybe
Leadership. Such men avoid grand mammals
Hungering for outdoor suppers; tasting,
S'mores, corn, coal-baked chops, 'tater boats,
Bits, pieces, toes, fingers, fleshy portions.

Afterwards, upland dwellers, dying out,
Morph from fear to fright as malls,
Housing, highways, factories, schools,
Displace mating, hunting, itching, gathering.
Then furries without new gene pools grasp
Human nibbles make poor nutrition, taste salty.

Like Stars in the Sky

The Jerusalem skyline, some tall buildings, mostly sandstone,
Occasional bright highway lights illuminating "important" folks.

Among the hills crowning this holiest of Earthly capitals, music, prayer,
Likewise, the good rhythms of everyday life, elevate dwellers and visitors.

Beneath the totality of such luminosity, under stars positioned by our Maker,
Darkness, memories of such savagery as ought not to be imaginable, grow rancid.

Not enough years ago, it was popular to embrace fear instead of faith,
To dog Am Yisrael wherever we settled, Europe sought quick fix; genocide.

Murder, maiming, rape, ghastly "scientific" experiments, in concert
Tormented our people, our lives, our unity, our hope for time forward.

Moshiach did not land soon enough; we became squeezed olives,
Our oil seeping even as entreating the Creator of the constellations.

Fernweh

Electronic images, posted in neat pockets of social media, sustain
A strange longing for real licorice, pigeon breasts neatly poached,
Also small intervals of cafuné.

It's not so much that Europe, or those crazy nights in Asia, took
Back palettes of irises, ranunculi, likewise dahlias, as if flowers
Acted like barometers for unrequited affections.

I no more experienced hiraeth than I felt deterred after pawning
The diamond, its matching earrings, gems you gifted me before
Hours of debauchery.

There's no firgun among man and wife when one gambols around
International centers while the other's left sorting laundry amongst
Inattentive ex-patriots.

My cravings were never filled by fresh bouquets or bright stones.
Your butterfly kisses, personal scent, sloppy hugs, alone, bestow
All necessary life basics.

Those Intricate Pastel Patterns

Those intricate pastel patterns,
Swirls, spots, other markings,
Resemble best select rodent-friendly
Moments, when cats get thwarted.

Small measures of violence,
That fill webs dangling succulent
Prey formed from clerks, clerics,
Pedestrian sorts, oft portend death.

Academic know-how remains
Impotent against crisply cool
Insurgents bent upon children
Suffering via "good" truncheons.

Other armaments, tools, devices
Fail to kill, leave footprints.
Such payoff, compromised, brings
Lethal, but innovative slayings.

Here, Pingo Sits:
An Intergalactic Placement of Sentiment

Here Pingo sits,
Not a second too more,
Cerebral gates, her realm to explore.

Their puzzle's her riddle,
Those high mentations, her ride,
To cosmic impasses strung up tight inside.

Fresh cranium bubbles,
Completely absence of love,
Confound her reliance on results, thereof.

The quandary, titanic,
The equation's bespoken insane,
Pointing, pondering just distorts what remains.

Thought krankens route freely,
Emotion's monsters can't synchronize.
(Discordance, infighting, is what those beasts prize.)

When old-fashioned hardships,
Astride odd, dear, defined friable parts,
Freeze, they perplex thinkers of middling smarts.

Munchkins Wearing Braids:
A High School Perspective

Munchkins wearing braids, as well as Kotex,
Fight over comic books, boys, nail lacquer,
Complain that squared cereal, garbage duty,
Bus fare prices pong, spin their fair heads.

Usually, while asking for money, such girls,
Forego trainings covering ancient ossuaries,
Choose, instead, to compete for places in track
And field, get crowned Homecoming Queen.

After all, adolescent excrescences, those open
Outgrowths of peer pressure, iffy grades, acne,
Coruscate alongside lockers, by cafeteria trays,
As well as in the midst of biology lab lessons.

Kamuros nearly to a one, those frenetic genera,
Skite on algebra, anyway succeed in acquiring
Sports heroes, student body presidents. Transfer
Students their minions, popularity their métier.

Candy Corn Castles

Candy corn castles, clotted cream mountains, ribboned girls, bright-buttoned boys,
All of the joys that might spin little known facts, within low fortifications' walls,
Elaborate small genealogical inventory.

Erstwhile, glittery parrots, lollipop trees, confectionary raindrops, monkeys, penguins,
Breezy promenades filled with shaping pots, weaving baskets, grieving snowflakes,
Build sagas from betrayal.

Gingerbread dancers, lacey tutus minus affiliated limbs, decrepit events, customs, chants,
Bud with sweet frogs, misty music, canvas, paper, cities of single-roomed buildings,
Hold fast simple multitudes as faltering standard bearers.

Cheshire cats, weird Alices, limits imposed by "healers," bejeweled, bespelled, alliances,
Veracities understood to evolve encased in iridium, copper, bronze, lead, or silver,
Climb blithely, nosedive, and die.

Sparrows, doves, even ravens, pink ponies trotted out in relatively kickshaw dinghies,
Tabs placed alongside human monsters, scrambled eggs in car crashes, pustules,
Reinforce notions nothing this side of foolhardy.

Giant creepy crawlies, magistrates, elevated past everyone's bees wax, busted stars,
The costume jewelry of condign consequences, decorative pieces gone bad,
Prolong suffering, add psychic pain.

Whining, parenthetically, sidling up to metal tools, rare weapons, seahorses, porcupines,
Poisons local battles' outcomes, resounding against pirates' palaces, glitter,
Portsg no supper.

Concurrently, cultivating wheat, barley, lentils, peas, inbred sheep, goats, cattle, hens,
Blocks of stone, bone, and wood, also cement, make shepherding too costly,
Cease brazened relationships of malevolent sorts.

Kings, high ranking clerics, bandits, perhaps belly dancers, jugglers, fifers, orcs, elves,
Gathered hamlets and villages' irregular trees, failing to overplay social doubts;
Shape ethics' hard chattels.

A Middle-Aged Mom's
Response to a Daycare Center's Shenanigans

Teetering on a stepstool, vying for penultimate, or best position,
At the local campus' daycare center, one chubby infant slipped.
The point nearest her face smiled blood, as did some linoleum.
Mama, unaware, two buildings away, spewed rhetorical mores.

Cultural anthropology, promoting the illusion of gender disparity,
In traditional religious groups, remains the framework employed
To: rationalize the rescue of earthworms from puddles, ice, snow,
Practiced suzerainty, and assess employer chirality/relative merit.

Matte yellow hummingbirds compete with iridescent purple ones;
My window box's lavender, parsley, also rosemary, blooms chime
Across valleys, appear worth feathery fights from crepuscular fey,
For sagging breasts, wrinkled skin, empty nests, insomniac nights.

We middle-agers lacking the sense to stay dumb, resume embracing
Waterlogged sentiments, even before Childhood Education majors,
Interns, hazard accidental death for any dear ones entrusted to them.
Bad habits, electronic distractions, sleep-deprived moments add up.

Seems, we wives tired of defending old, overstretched stomachs,
Complain little about unannounced bathroom intentions, prefer
Donating kidneys, ignore parenting troubles, tribulations, stress,
Pose for life drawing classes, eat French fries with cheese gravy.

The largest sort of shame, cheap, poor quality, otherwise tawdry,
Packages social goods such that tattling on grade school buddies,
Those kids deigning to rub flour paste on teachers' coat hangers,
Forces us to smirk facetiously, cast off helplessness' tears, shrug.

A Flat, Antithetical Season

Sherry-colored pious miniatures sing
Sparkling dollops of laughter, of spleen,
While calendar-dependent appetites ring
Cookie-cutter eddies of archaic dreams.

Stomping, they turn air puffs,
Base, beloved, or otherwise,
To masquerades turkey-stuffed
From merriment of possibility.

Beware children! Return! Respond!
Effervescents contour false hopes.
In ho-hum, humble crazies' homes,
Within some managers' narratives.

Split cellos still can fake,
Symphonic wonderment,
Dropping substantial notes
Until listeners apologize.

Jeopardy shepherds mistletoe,
Anger's not in words; reindeer
Prefer that their friends know
That hoof beats can be heard.

Racing Bikes: Childhood Memories

Down
 The
  Hill,
   Around
    We
Spin.
Racing bikes, who might win?

Streamers flying,
Neighbors vying,
Our speeds can seem so death-defying!

Slowly, care-ful-ly, we
s   t   o   p,   sprawl, relax.
Drink some pop.

With sunshine bright,
Plus song birds' tweet,
Racing's what we do each week.

La! This Joy that is Spring

Singularly singing fragility's often bloomed flowers,
Extending bits of trickling, twinkling, simple hours,
Through filigree branches, wispy, fragile, rosy pink,
Rotund, effervescent reflections of fleecy thinking,
Mouth open, arms encircling, welcoming the season.

My reasoning comes, goes, subway cars transversing
Ticky-tacky's eternal yellow violet billboard curses.
Our city vibrates loud all shades of tarnished silver
Places, where we once picked tart apples, pilfered
Cigarette papers, hairclips, drugstore penny candy.
Purloining beer distributors' recycled goods meant
Neighborhood petrol stations, ice cream halls lent
Wiggling, half-dead raccoons, layers of usual trash,
Pulp magazines, loitering pubescents, minors rashly
Coupled, disentangled, but forgetting their condoms.

In our childhood, "baby-sized" cones cost two cents,
Stealing erasers from Kmart allowed us to augment
Winter's tatty allowances, sitter cash, paper routes.
Until vastly different sorts of "friends," thereabouts,
Menacingly, brutally uprooted free-growth saplings.
Running away, throughout most ferocious winters,
Did nothing to chill enormous hands from sintering
Small heads. Hence, we tattled, spit, bullied, pushed,
Broke crayons, graffitied walls, got high on cush, as
Well as whited-out trendy girls' shiny yearbook faces.

Angry children miss the point of purchased feelings,
When mentally ill parents, dirtying kiddies, conceal
Normalcy's construction of familial safety, then lash
Again, again, again at weaker others, or, unabashedly,
Vivisect hard-won developmental milestones, stars.
Cigarettes hung from lips, flasks tucked not-so-neatly.
Some teens spread human waste on walls, repeatedly,
Scream by means of truancies, pregnancies, overdoses,
Struggle opposing undeservedly extraordinary ghosts,
Occasionally, belly up to despair, depression & death.

So, la! This joy that is spring, this item of solar celebration,
This recovering of sweets fallen from grocery depots bins,
This refolding of sweaters left strewn 'round bright stores,
This tribute to woods, streams, all the imagined outdoors,
Culls sealskin-stuffed animals possessed of dark, pin eyes,
Amasses memories prized from puddles, remnants, tatters.
Yes, Gloria, each starfish pitched back to the sea does matter.
Improving a life, if not mine, fetches a measured solace.
Transcends canons, beliefs, limits, childhood promises,
Settles the record this season of year, scrutinizes serenity.

Peach Pit Bridges

Stacking bits, pits of our lost decade's
Nights spent wondering on preserving
Memories, can't bring that time again.

Those truths of husks, shells, glumes,
Such leftover recollections augment,
Strengthen few abandoned moments.

Glancing back yields few newborn suns,
Guarantees no former joys will, perhaps,
Eclipse today, then, linger, elsewise stay.

Nursery songs remain standing, hanging
Around this parent's head, lodging solid
Rinds, reordering, and blighting bygones.

Today, you're married, set with child.
I suck, thus, at piled seeds, arils, hulls,
Gleaning fruit from stone, once more.

Littoral

When situated on the shore of quiet lakes,
Most solicitous spouses' purview covers
Takedowns.

Consider that effusive give and take seldom
Bucks at frank sentiment, preferring seagull
Rotations.

Misplaced oceanic birds, akin to wives looped
By gadgets, regularly endure hardships whilst
Deckled.

Accouchement's nothing relative to raising
A comrade; many men prefer offhandness'
Glissando.

Hence, following decades washed from coasts,
Heartlands offer no resistance to obverse lees,
Or humbugs.

Juliet Capulet, Her Nurse, and the Moon

"Lunar Lady of the night,
What evil you yet play,
On darlings' simple, drifting hearts.
By desires that you sway.

Lesser sun, you cursed fiend,
Now lift your blight from me,
This fair child's unfussy love's
Not meant as victory."

"What is it dear, that strong unrest,
I hear beneath your singular sill?
Strange words you're bold to confess,
Your face gleams stranger still."

"Granny Dear, it hurts me here,
Such nasty, sharp, bright pain.
Perhaps it's from the evening air,
I won't complain, again.

(I'm not too new to know or guess
What sighs, what lurks beyond.
By what odd means secrets unfold,
Or lovers carry on.)"

"Hush, Dear One, quiet now,
Rest your head, pose calm.
Morning's just a little while
'fore shelter from the storm."

"But Nursie Sweet, it stays as true
The moon's warriors, her knaves,
Work fairy tales, nothing more;
Only maidens can be brave.

I've fallen from my ledge, out there,
I've tripped into a cote,
Where beasts rip up the chaste, they tear.
There's no way to get out."
"Little Dove, don't speak of such.
You'll continue good and pure.
No winning comes from darkened thoughts,
From reaching past your door."

"Almost Mother, it's too late
To call back horses fled,
I cry with night, will know the day.
I die upon my bed.

I pledged my troth, I gave my word.
I'm broken through and through
I have no breath, no honor left,
Without Sir Montague."

Babes in Buggies

For sensation reminiscent of gamboge treatments, we incline toward
Ricocheting entrails to points ordinarily beyond main-belt asteroids.
In the case of war, it's recommended to shave beards, compel bribes,
Run to the nearest interstellar quay, eat lots of pickle & butter sarnies.
More decisively, rhetoric that manufactures its own healable wounds,
No manner the manner of clevises installed, makes fresh social media
Rather than solves living history or conjures hippocrases. Go figure.
Editors point out poor gendarmes; moneyed impulses befriend them.

"Magics" like apportation, enamor imaginary hedgehogs, bile, also chickweed,
Support community circumstances. Azure-haired chanters, many coque hackles,
Stick their tongues out, fart, as well as push worldly fingers into shared morass.
Cometary cultural changes, fire, brimstone, celestial fury, creates labile affects.
Among alleged aggrieved innocence, failing escaping horrid mau-mau voicings,
Spiritual sabatons bait us. Folks past rehabilitation guide silently, mostly. Folks
Implore exploding, knifing, murdering, towering gossip, challenging academics.
In wrestling meat from living animals, those folks present heinous predilections.

Babes in buggies, ordinarily, capture hardly any paparazzos' notice,
Yet stepping over wounded, in the street, as gutters run full of bits,
Brings all manners of camcorders, habanera plantations, flashbulbs,
Bolts of grosgrain, intractable prose, and strongly measured poetics.
Convenience store clerks, poorly ranking clerics, kings, polar bears,
Best drawn out friends' properties (Blunt Street's been designated
incapable of micturating alongside of existent banister workforce—
up till now, political sollerets nonetheless offer limited protection.)

Along with the Doll

Too hastily, along with the doll tossed last year,
She rooted in familial stock, made pride in heritage.
Her harbor of helpful bits, that social sanctuary, mental
Vicinity, where bedrooms of critical thinkers dared not stalk,
Remained a place in which ambitions became canceled, snuffed.

Such a gal's imperfect blathering of truth recalled no
Ongoing telepathic events else even fiduciary appreciations;
There, parental exaltations waited, as did isolated, yet fashionable
Ways and means for completing chores, excluding gleaning "hakobe,"
In other words, not counting the gathering, dicing of "star chickweed."

Experiences around her spreadsheet, likewise, most oft separated
Squishy private drops from former suffered thirsts. Rubrics mattered.
Girly lingered far from ignorance concerning: sentience justifications,
Snarls in spider webs, antique musettes, horses suffering spavin, azoturia,
Marital infidelities, somebody's wee kitten pulled from the loch, also botulism.

Similarly, she stored vegetables and whole grain crackers,
Utilizing tiny plasticware, proving entertainment for some kids,
Forget to fold laundry, sweep floors, fancy most dubious enterprises.
Family function necessitated pairing individual slices, some greens, rice.
Pulp, charif, wise guy remarks, dead flowers, also laconic conversations.

On balance, horrible, chemically-laden grocery store shampoo,
Ordinarily obfuscated by general domestic mayhem, else coupons,
Lacked no power to remove lice, even to clean properly, smell good.
Without associated fortifications, her toddlers stumbled rose, stumbled.
"Time out," minus toys, continued on as important in family life, survival.

Unnatural Considerations

As a Salute

As a salute to a landed institute, a short story, which, initially, seems like blue
    prose, might
Get cleaned up, perhaps altered, or, mayhap, eventually, over time, corroborate
    crazy tosh.

"Little smiles," over grownup goings-on, moreso, can't compare to verse that starts
    to rant,
Then manifests, in its final form, unfashionable diatribes decrying genuine party
    problems.

Sometimes, creative writing professors, excepting the top tier, are paid poorly,
    relative to
Instructors in computer science, business, engineering, i.e. "profitable" academic
    sectors.

See, mitigating cultural "woes," rather than insisting that "afflictions" continue on
    conveniently,
Habitually obliges middle managers overlook opportunities to accumulate
    promised materials.

Accordingly, spectators weigh leaving behind prejudice, but bringing along tourist
    Dollars,
Euros, and Yen, to all famous corners of commercial enterprises; charity yields
    small profit.

Perspicacious others, in any case, appreciate that base nature drives folks to seek
    ready money.
Modern rhetoric's "job" remains yielding genotoxicity to collective understandings
    of "good."

Flipping Houses

"Flipping houses," peculiarly, used to mean "working on investments, taking
Dividends." Today, all the same, mollycoddling regularly transports forward
Hackneyed gifts. As well, disregarding attempts to engineer pit bosses' cries,
Brings, at best, questionable earnings.

Realize, any shortfall in companionable devotion, in that sickly sweet feeling
Of imposture, of believing deceptive comforts wrought by upholding science,
Outplays operatic showers, potentially, this flank of the Mississippi. Deficits
Stymie super intelligent graduate students, also slugs.

Contrarians may well profess how embracing dear subject matter makes good
Results, not unhappy endings. They're wrong. Note; conveying designs costs,
Personal integrity, tuition, maybe virginal rights, parasols, plus guano sachets.
Success will never be as not cheap as scotch.

Ostranennie

It's not a cup, but a strange ship, a rocket seen by our errant children.
They comprehend that the towel, nearby, belongs beyond deep space.
They grasp how jarring music, once beloved, sends signals far away.
As well, they see the cat, which "watches birds," summons troops
To repositioning, to surmount more than common sparrows' lanes.

Hence, those youngsters, some altruistic, some otherwise, fabricate,
Tell us tall folks the whys of games, though all along truly secreting
Green men, gray ladies, beasts with horns of salt and diamond eyes,
Wide-reaching ray guns, nearly invisible transporters, crazy wealth
Measured in matchbook covers, tulip bulbs, also winter tangerines.

In a particular smultronställe, where bears, crows, foxes congregate,
No small amount of rasasvada overcomes intentional visitors. Some
Overly curious government agents misstep their limits, die sighting
How, beneath oaks and elms, bliss sprinkled from alien limbs glows.
Web surfers neglect to check the darkened corners of oceans, forests.

Most officials' acatalepsy partitions them safe from wonders wrought
By star breakers, their companion dragons, trolls. Rarely commoners
Allow space for spiritual growth or extraterrestrial sehnsucht. Grasp,
We seek coffee shops, corner taverns, fishing ponds, watery, gezellig
Places. Past vacation fliers, auto ads, launch parties, we're truly blind.

Save for nefelibatas, preschoolers, domestic pets, feral birds, no one
Acknowledges the coexistence of outworlders. In the end, metanoia's
Accessible merely to stouthearted or open-minded citizens. Typical
Swarms, on this sphere, is lacking gumption necessary to contemplate
Any dérive. No orenda, no matter how exciting, flicks our existence.

Odd as Cows in Fur-Lined Trees

Deconstructing the global milieu gets odd
As cows seeking safety in fur-lined trees;
Bovine sleep standing, while folk lounge
Somnolent on sofas, davenports, couches.

Political changes appear best when whisked, diced,
Then spiced up with media criticism. Alternatively,
A common coquelicot of language mayhap appease
Foreign appetites bent on ruling acreages not theirs.

Fortunately, it's possible for current events
To sufficiently disturb us into remembering;
(we're the needed ultimate bulwark against
Hatred and discrimination directed at Jews.)

Womanizing linguistics, word salad, hallucinations,
Invasive social orders, intergenerational rebellion,
Colonial wars, disturbing instances of power plays;
Ain't nothing vernal relative to international racism.

Scurrilous

Making, spreading scandalous claims that damage,
Seems the intentional work, not just of witches, but
Likewise starlets, amateur athletes, most politicians.

It's nearly antinomical just how badly big boys, girls
Behave when antagonizing over propriety or fortune.
Wads of green paper manage to yield sundry sclerae.

Even religion's portcullises seem little match against
Structures built from funded tesserae, also cameras.
When not Internet aces, would-bes settle for movies.

Teenage Infatuation

I'd write you a song, I'd send you a poem.
Your letters of love, I'd cherished at home.

I'd carry your picture, your smile, in my heart.
Fill hankies, tear tissues, each time we need part.

My mind spirals to delight from your words,
I'd savor your kisses, even those just inferred.

Such glittery feelings, your presence would bring,
Such blushing to cheeks, to limbs, to odd things.

I believe that you're magic, that maybe you'd lift
My outlook, my sorrow, my yesterday's rift.

He refused me the sky, denied me the clouds.
Darkened my dreams, shamed me often, aloud.

As his twin, you would know how to play angel flutes,
Our coupling would zing (of course, you're truly cute.)

The Willing Face of Corporate Chemistry

The willing face of corporate chemistry continues to abuse power, to lower
Charges brought against assart bullies liberating bosses from investigation.
Captured partners, even types pleasing to look at, die one by one, as it goes.

Grasp, money's successful hooks no longer astonishing workers or media,
Whether or not demises occur suddenly, else linger like bad drain cleaners
In toilets, sinks, bathtubs, reservoirs, all contrary to healthy living. Stinks!

Members of most sales forces buck competitively-priced services, equally
Deign to advertise, as superior products, less-than-industry standard, tripe
While accruing adoration purchased across untruths, mendacities, deceits.

They purchase consumer love via quiltbag politics, possible epigenetic
Changes, place their findings in "academic" journals of no true appeal.
Five year-old-styled wisdoms can't ever parallel weathered certainties.

A Fixity of Posture

Catalepsy's initially regarded as
Socially uncouth, likewise akin
To burping, abiding borborygmus,
Eating lukewarm pottage, sipping
Brackish water, embracing math by way of infinitesimals.

See, déraciné, that dire displacement
Experienced by swathy folks, intent
Not on assimilating, but on capture,
Routes' subjective sense perceptions;
Most bonkbusters discomfort grannies, distress preachers.

It's insufficient just to chop potatoes
Into wee tetragons if deracinating—
Meddlers require knives, sticks, any
Weapon, really, that fits together the
Pieces, whose components stanchion outworlder functions.

As we embrace rendition, all manner
Of terror attempts groaking unsullied
Blatteroons, talking awhile adjusting
Headsets. Politicians, basically, can
Apostrophize 'til dawn—professional accountability wilts.

Reflect, we're no smellfungi, just dull
Citizens cognizant that monokinis, or
Burkinis, mightn't be for showcasing
Female form, increased sensitivity to
Misogyny, protecting women from all ingrained prejudice.

Designs, even now, are harvested from
Lists, from geometry else trigonometry
From men too unsophisticated to grasp
Concepts correlating rates, slopes, pain,
Save no one, won't render their communication consequential.

Viz, most noumenal (not phenomena)
Surround profoundly fused moments.
Elsewise, practicing non-judgment on
Sad environments encourages engaging
Scary places; Benin, Burundi, Mauritania, Gabon, and Dijbouti.

Doxing

Searching for, plus publishing, on Facebook, Instagram, maybe also
Twitter, various reserved bits, pieces, remarks, images, gossips, can
Form additional parades of allegorical, pudendum-like indiscretions.

Unlike airport or factory hawker centers, the Internet's no place for
Dubious samples, their amazing flavors notwithstanding. Crossing
Appendages ill-suffices to ward off equals. Deleting recovers amity.

Accordingly, morons, snake oil salesmen, disparate malevolent folk,
Get rubricked as prancing, distributing rumors, tittle-tattles, buzzes
Consisting of bosh and trash, as we simples reinvestigate propriety.

Rubbernecking from Bus Stops

When rubbernecking from bus stops,
Riders mistake sidewalks and puddles,
Suspend required discipline to gawk,
Allowing morbid curiosity's fixation
To weigh the degree of their craning.

It appears, most often, that sociopaths,
Whether driven by compulsion, rage,
Self-entitlement, lean to discourteous.
When accomplishing tasks, they fail
To control ambition, self-image, ego.

Also, souls forget that hedgehogs nibble,
Yet, an entire prickle's pecks can wound,
Matched proposals' macaronic audiences
Notwithstanding; Uchronia stays fiction
Until palomino ponies outplay unicorns.

Superiors' Specifications

She was paid well to dispatch a few exotic creatures,
Scaly, slimy beasts, some mottled, even cold-blooded,
Pets of corporate lawyers plus certain beggar proxies.

Beyond the teeth, claws, many toxins, outworlders
Remained unthreatened, persisted as trade partners;
Intellectual prowess usually wins over most worlds.

Few leads owning rumblegumption raised objections.
They, likewise, employed beings as narratives' actors,
Elsewise exiled folk to the dated Kingdom of Sikkim.

Hence, denizens, all a fluster, felt deep swivet, buckled.
(Unlike dodgy balladeers' products, Old World animals
Agendas traffic sluggishly, massacred fiends excepted.)

Political correctness' vulgar nature, no matter precisely
The soft things rubricked as "ideologically dangerous,"
Washes up in despair and attempts passé civic function.

At least such drivel successfully impacts idiots, often
Contextualizes sentiment, nickel and dimes stomach-
Churning-linked advocacy, kinkajou's prehensile tails.

Elsewhere, underhanded producers infuse manuscripts,
Mask worthy messages as void of critical or creative
Motes (both deliberately plus mistakably). We're sunk.

Duplicitous, Bleeding Hearts and Vagabonds

Powers and values differ among troupes
Such that transitional stages of processes,
Except for folks with benevolent miens,
Frequently entail sanguinary goings-on.

Nonetheless, the ballad of the celebrated,
Expensive, anti-tank, rustproof keychain,
All apotheositic in its precipitous ending,
Overhauled recognized civic conventions.

This tale's nisi jurisdiction, its elliptical
Expression, went unchallenged because
Our verge of dairy cow pastures, & our
Fringe, arable lands, crofts, remain vital.

Intrinsically, our most arduous defense,
Ever contended by our office, detonated,
Discharging chipped porcelain façades,
Spotty overhauls of cultural gnashnabs.

Thereafter, the public lapsed from sublime
To trivial, in prioritizing our preparations
For contingencies blistering, maybe colder.
Lamentably, we frittered away much time.

Today, friends still chafe from concomitant
Strictures of past cooperative promotions.
Wealth, enviable providence, largely, halts
Us, excluding beef farming, swine health.

At best, men log gratuity hours examining
Abnormal exists. It's possible, eusociality
Will prevail, will provide fictional reads,
Will make utter losers erstwhile winners.

Laudanum Tinctures

That observable, illuminated potion of codeine, also morphine,
Eases ecchymoses (plus the pain from other kinds of bleeding).
Inversely, fervid restorations can't counteract horrid prolepses,
Regardless of iterative nature or stints passed in transhumance.

Plague victims, whether microbially stricken or of broken hearts,
Seem to pule until the very querulous sounds they radiate become
Sublunary, that is, until losing all reference to improved spheres,
All attachment to aeonic worlds, to prior, nobler portions of life.

To wit, from my window, I watched authorities take a woman away
She had already ceased to clobber, having otherwise made her home
Disorderly. No one would admit that bedizened beauties, regularly
Sought proximity to that crone's medicines or wanted her wisdoms.

The lady's universe spun without batteries; no electrical device ran.
Rather, the heavens' selfsame reprobate agents created her energy,
Helped swirl her tops, rotate her planets, gyrate her odd sepulchral
Entities over many broad chiliads, close to many speckled systems.

Galactic travel's an imprecation. Simply, space farers die rapider
Than tortoises hunted, rapaciously, for soup or accessories' parts.
Even when drugged, star sailors manage to visit family no matter
How rugose their viscera become, how despondent their darlings.

Human stoma can open involuntarily, letting out horrid, chthonic
Seepage, dark or otherwise evil minxes, indications of pestilence,
Make innocents leave behind baldrics, despite youngins' desires.
Similarly, stomas dry up orgone, cull miseries amongst sufferers.

Precocity, especially in desultory, displaced aliens, happenings
Weird alembics, automated decay, machine-driven tosh, deliria.
As threnodies resonate in dreary towers, pilfered stellar palfreys
Flee, allow stridor to echo off chamber walls, flesh to fall away.

Of Bandoliers and Boulangeries

Through select apertures, added marvels flow.
Resembling American Revolution pamphlets,
Supplementary crusades bring no bombshells;
They merely galvanize election-biased minds.

Elsewise, uninspired folks' numinous passages
Meander, use untraceable accounts, urge peer
Suspicions to materialize in software crafted
For punters seeking spontaneous contractions.

The minute desultorily, lost paramours blubber,
Illicit emoluments enable them to keep minions.
Their exoneration from sordid acts establishes
Contrived trusts plus easily proven prejudices.

See, generosity, wisdom, honor, ain't mundanes'
Greatest powers. Simple sprogs oughtn't excuse:
Foozled larcenies of dotards, taking toffees off
Babies, screaming through neighborhood lungs.

By avoiding familial visits to prison wards, folks,
Mayhap, skip dreary encounters, random bathos,
Dubashes' bridleways besides spoiled sourdough-
Sucking down rehabilitation en plein air struggles.

Further, kids doomed to lives filled with doodly
Software, idleness, health scares, clan woes, all
Clichés journeying to contentious arenas, catch
No possibilities of parole or of basic pasturage.

Au courant rulings' retalitorily pirate files filch
Optimism from pessimists, comparably contort
Sundry innocent citizens into implacable mobs,
Repurpose institutions as sophisticated rangolis.

No More Notice

When self-entitled persons become sufficiently savvy to use aliases with dear cohorts,
Or to exercise anthropomorphic protagonists when rounding with non-human chums,
Questions get asked.

Note, pulling back from stroking cute kittens, domesticated alpacas, moist chinchillas,
Resonates as alarming among larvae, worshippers of deltaic altars, and galaxy junkies.
PoMo remains a limited aesthetic.

Beneath the hills of Kobarid, where spiny mammals' misdeeds rival those of frat boys,
Luggage weight restrictions, dobros, sanitary pads, and ska saxophone music resonate.
Such laxity brings returns on investments.

"Feminist Prose and Poetics" and "Female Society" conflated with trinket courses
Vis-à-vis curt acceptances literal observations, dairy cow herds, fluffy petards rot.
(Only rebuffed academics like those assessments.)

Left to popular marches, stratagem arrange quinellas, mark decals on all flanks of boxes,
Color vehicular trunks, crack gaolers' spines, play go fish, gawk at HUDs, hum off-key.
Fame gamers sunder peers, teach less, worry more.

Girls, gone bad from too many ballet lessons, swivet grand populations, fight brothers,
Get lost on either side of the inspired divide or in diminutive microwaves, utilize paws.
They rely on shared noospheres to pass alone messages.

Chance inclusions spend excessive epochs with household substances belonging to fey,
Elbowing passengers, eating watermelon, kissing equerries, staying awake round noon.
Unctuous others are often willing to count planemoses beyond Neptune.

Folks, whose parents are charity and myopia, don't tolerate laughter, postpartum moods.
For them, engaging in research invites anticipated results vis-à-vis unanticipated events.
Revenants make good reports as does frolicking among giant pods of narwhals.

If only studios featuring kitchenettes could be forgotten in favor of enjoying ships' chefs,
Cooking privileges, all journey long, upheavals would go unattempted, pups would sleep.
Eidolons' dance instruction, on decks under sloppy clouds, would quickly sell out.

Not Loving the CDC's Word Ban

Banning lexicon is old school, like censoring: Brave
New World, Of Mice and Men, To Kill a Mockingbird,
All Quiet on the Western Front, Persepolis, Candide.

Term lists ought not to proscribe equality. Municipal
Boldness, realized thru rhetorical vehicles, exposure,
Evidence-based forms of unusual platforms, obliges.

Note, diversity increases awareness. Idiolects encourage
More than "7 Words You Can't Say on TV," safeguard
Against certain groups' entitlement superseding justice.

It's known that hate names cause populations' collapse,
Suffer destitute folk to kowtow to discrimination—no
Matter peccadilloes of handcuffed language, judgment.

Not any science-based "verities" belong before liberties;
Even "slogging masses" need determine whether simple
Speech or magniloquence best supplies privation, tastes.

Eliminating descriptions like "transgender" oddly vogues
Archaic anopisthographs, triggers "modern" medicine to
Become "politics as usual," rather than flowering mutiny.

Critical thinking appears in the fetus period, towered over
By budget deliberations, Capitol Hill say-so, selfish goals.
Nevertheless, championing communication remains noble.

Assiduity

Both the university teacher and that random member of humanity
Responded to diverse situations, embraced people of ethnicities,
Taught them not to: fear poodles, impregnate minors, spread lies;
Rather, compere welcome parties, serve miso soup, gassy water.

Mostly, the two espoused that folk involved with wary kindness,
No matter the cobblestones running through their kitchens, could
Love, generate families. In addition, the brace promised friends'
Tenderness brings aerial stunts, divvies Padparadscha sapphires.

When answering other peoples' problems, the pair succeeded as
Heroes, of sorts. Their landing pages filled with adorations from
Numerous followers seeking tactics for exposing stifling bosses.
So, the duo charged the cost of their projects' labor and delivery.

As well, the twinned thinkers increased their social standing via
Discourse, availed men of odd, antiquated mail collection boxes,
Enabled certain mental orbits to recycle. Society, it seemed, liked
Thickly misted organized crime, kept alive numbing mind games.

Select Taxons of Behavior

Some taxons of behaviors line up at troughs for evening meats,
Ignore those pastures where green grasses grow dolorous feels,
Stay far from creeks tendering wee dissonances' bowed angers,
Stride clear of salt licks gingered up with prolix egocentrisms.

Alternatively, some rush to gulp down sweet ruminations, plus any
Inferences of information yielding pleasant thoughts, good actions,
Random forms of kindness. Accordingly, such hurry to avoid most
Materialisms. Likewise, publics circumvent fissures of wickedness.

Realize, the lushest forbs make mouthfeel that emulates decency.
Savvy people connect with family, aid friends, benefit affinities.
They generally sanction apprenticing selves to charitable doings,
To devoting lifetimes to trying to fix the world, even just a little.

Welkin

Virtual narrative places the firmament, the blue crystal ceiling,
As protecting rabbits, dolphins, societies, manufacturing hope,
Inspiring our reworking for skep-like security, above, beyond.

Moral drogues, built by "important" societies, never referenced
During elections, coup d'états, provide no understandings, give
Over heaps of significant, mass marketed containers, longueurs.

Unless folks employ binoculars, kites, perambulation at picnics,
Big "champions" continue yielding sops, 'til standards plummet
Like fidelity or fresh methods of opposing skeptics' hypergolics.

When gobbling up best treats, those yokels count to seventy-two,
Remain didactic in their sameness, spout all manner of universal
Epitaphs, whether quaggy, salacious, or otherwise objectionable.

Only handfuls of compassion service providers, well past teen
Years, ever supply constructive feedback when stuck on topics
Such as: architectural refinements, binturong tail lengths, truth.

Contemporary culture's tropes, designated by leopards, monkeys,
Longhorns, don't become news darlings since taboo, racist, sexist,
Narrow-minded words merely sell well if writers play as therapists.

See, media pups hang back, enjoy, without "pleases," "thank-yous"
Much anaphor, at the same time as most of their littermates wean;
Worrying about intruders is no longer the demesne of diminutives.

Simultaneously, skilled word players mix emotive with scientific
Language, send prolepses of doom, creates more jumble, attempt
Bettering society toward achieving redemption, reaching rapture.

Prioritizing Quintessential Deeds

Prioritizing quintessential deeds,
Makes mawkish prose copulate
With people, also weird critters.

Maybe, Mars will become habitable
At such a time, dating sweet-looking,
Artless aliens, chanced at salad bars.
Will be fine, no longer scandalous.

For now, fictitious persons can't talk
Back, press on past existent oubliettes
Try outlying, barely accessible zones.
The avoid scary, vital prevarication,
Boluses, punters, surplus iconic bits.

Intergalactic assemblages are trendier
Than paperbacks celebrating discord.
For various reasons, exploring stars'
Electronic pulses might prove puerile
If backed by telescopes, microscopes,
Bonus instruments of medieval torture.

Gelatinous slugs are rumored to enjoy
Barking nations' rights to antinomies,
Fueling greenhouse fears, tempering
Mannerisms, possibly escalating old
Clarion orders to uncompromisingly
Revisit planets' exertions at patency
Among obsequious hominid visitors.

Presently, space gangs claim no surety
Of safety from limy leeches, sour dogs.
Swearing off unnatural spheres' spins,
Fighting off omnifarious inapt elements
Handy in negotiating for orchids, films,
Shared graphics, broods full of alacrity,
Stippled servant, interspecies principles,
Copious fraternities flouted over comets.

An Ecological Society's Invitation to International Protocol

Conversational ergativity often silences whys/wherefores,
In terms of morphosyntax or especially per plain civility.
Similarly, cameraless photography's impressive for starts,
Weddings, birthdays, Bar Mitzvahs, but not for stretches
Before craven, bibulous louts swarm public dining rooms.

Sometimes, in the practice of discovering escape routes,
Notable exceptions notwithstanding, pretty drivers prefer
Puzzling out the sorts of beasts that drool over doorknobs,
Eat watercress for luncheon (without flossing), elsewise
Posset, hack up furballs, eject air onto sanitary surfaces.

Most medicos' restarted efforts toward presidential praise,
Slake drunkards' thirst, fill bottles of hope, permeate small
Minds, relocate where no brassy folks challenge puissance.
They're effective in routing apoplectic assistant managers,
Documentary film directors, random sous chefs, bunglers.

Elsewise, foozling's a forgotten art sunk in big reservoirs.
Elision, not the coexistence of sundry probable meanings,
Impacts tourism in Salamanca, in New York, in Amarillo.
Familial needs juxtaposed personal ones craft craquelures,
Social polysemy, slaking intellectual libidos, and bad puns.

When prosecutors succeeded in verifying, pro tem, selfish
Profiteers' nature, not a soul loses out on future abundance.
Enemies, who ordinarily might support stagnate conditions
Urge no successful hashing out of very altruistic pathways;
Advanced enmity paradigms eviscerate little smiles always.

Twinkle Stinking Little Star

Twinkle stinking little star,
You evil nighttime fiend,
Ill-results are all you want
From our domestic scene.

We won't yield to gold beacons
Bend toward a brackish throne,
Capitulate to your sinful whims,
Won't yield our hearth or home.

Cosmos-style complexities
Might exude us in foul dirt,
Yet your malevolence ways
Won't mark as greatest hurt.

Beyond ceilings' flicked light
Dwell noble hearts and souls.
A feeble, criminal blueprint,
In contrast, ain't that bold.

The Table Where They Had Been Seated

The table, where they had been seated, was left a mess
By strings of infidelities, French fries, ketchup, coffee,
"Cheerful" existence conflicted with unsatisfying sex,
A generous income, popular media pages, shimmering
Status-levels, imported nonmotorized vehicles, sloths.

Most stretches, her ex-husband, no exemplar of gender
Equanimity, invited, to that woman's wheeled paradise,
Fractious people (disregarding his lacking ownership).
Saying not much while silently communicating, shark
Wound entanglements, drizzled Champaign on the sly.

Rather than enter his clinch, his erstwhile waxed splenetic,
Demanding, in exchange for using her pricy conveniences,
Lots of hush money, parapet gifts, numerous inducements.
Plus, her bogotas got insured against hazardous alliances.
Critters lacking opposable digits, hussies, were outlawed.

Additionally, as long as he stayed on payroll, applicants
Could neither clap nor smile, nor buffet imaginations via
Bosh, cheap perfume, further "neighborly" expurgations.
Else, that bedroom troubadour would be dismissed, sans
Review boards reimbursing his borrowed doctoral cape.

In the end, her gravelly visage replaced his brazen bliss,
Brought countless awkward substitutions for permanent
Subsidies, whisked away donations secreted from artful
Visitors, completed tasks as pundits could no longer aid
That idiot, who was encumbered worse than TSA agents.

Shrewdness Derived from an Excess of Disquiet

His shrewdness derived from an excess of disquiet.
See, reality bites. Wounds reverberate. There exist
Sharp teeth willing to clamp down fully.

Darkness fetches fatigue, dryness, discouragement,
Overall emotional depletion, also small uglinesses,
Which sprout midmornings.

Bank accounts become the least of interpersonal worries.
It's as nothing to wear out antiquated microfilm readers,
To otherwise rid mental libraries of "old rubbish."

She would mindlessly stick her head inside the hoary monster
If her act resulted in their once more fumbling among daisies,
Being gawked at by passersby.

Still, their involvement called forth too many litigious knots.
Jumping trains no longer found them outside liminal notions
Like "entitlement," "well-paid work."

Sometimes, we're unable to countenance tech consultants,
To brazen out collective death, to stay the course against
Local and not-so-local business bludgeons.

Ultimately, she never learned his name, his Social Security
Number, address, LinkedIn moniker, dungeon avatar, beer.
His identity remained her guess.

He became yet another cozen, latest fellow lacking bona fides
One supplementary process of combining and refining dashes
All elegiac in their authenticity.

The Ways in Which We Puttered

When outmoded enough to care for community mothers, we counted
The routes they puttered in gardens, discarding placid, rainy day work
As balderdash-type business, only university scholars should jab wet
Dirt, sow in contentious grounds, attempt impossible, verdant growth.

Consider that godlets, their funders, utilize superficialities to unionize,
Seedpods to avoided ceding losses or relinquishing winnings, cuttings
To hold contrary relationships tethered to social machinations, formal
Paperwork to link collusive compliments to archaic, ductile archways.

Punitive adults never posture shared strictures' hush-hush evidence;
Rather, they promote content via social media, also friendly courses.
Less than cheerfully, they gambit rhetorical goals engineered by fey.
Granted, most establishments tire of defending complaints all hours.

Subsequently, laughter embarrasses crones, severs aged connections,
Causes grandmas to lose sleep, babies to cry out, lovers to toss, turn.
It's better to collect visible belly button lint or to ram eyes with pens
Than watch demolished dreams, hopes, fabulations for mere minutes.

Sanctimonious champions limit their purview to select skerries, keep
To safe geographic "wonders." Erstwhile victors simply shrug, break
Old-style phones, then apprentice to become lorry drivers, shepherds.
Too frequently, we discount the worth of drool, diminish snot's value.

If we'd conducted sounder research on strawberry trees, we might yet
Realize that surveillance, well used, may well bluster fiduciary satiety.
On balance, in cultures of robust men, pathetic women entrepreneurs
Sneer; peripheral appraisals carry weight, paid fees remain important.

Tomorrow, in double dug rows, additional renditions, those rucked up
Aspirations, will flower then fade. Infamously missing husbands will
Return, bovids will request milking. Running off to Canada will seem
Prudence as will jinking the sentiments of our hallowed grandmothers.

Conclusion: Paper and Kindred Devices

Paper holds no boundaries,
Feels no hate, bows no discrimination,
Reaches out, touches far flung imaginations,
Deeply piercing hearts, especially when flying to Podgorica.

Words impede only where leaves, shiny bugs,
Marshmallow fluff, oboluses, airlines tickets, dark skies,
'neath chocolate bushes, mooless cows, in fear, fail to multiply,
Any prenatal gatherings, misguided "benefactors," or "peace lovers."

Bands of Ukrainian executives scold days
Possessed of cats, illusory hedgehogs, birdseed,
Yield no part of winnings, clutch corporate greed,
Trample literary themes, genres, publishing circumstances.

The second orchestral chair's mostly a hat rest.
Budapest's bank managers, coeds, homeboys, housewives,
Live to weed highway meridians, to add spelunking to their lives,
Europeans still cough up fur balls, skip novels' middles, try to elude taxes.

Credits:

"A Fixity of Posture." *Bindweed*. Apr. 2019.

"A Flash Mob for Holiday Shoppers." *vox poetica*. Dec. 2012.

"A Flat, Antithetical Season." *Sarasvati*. Jan. 2010.

"A Meadow Morning's Limitations." *Danse Macabre*. Apr. 2013.

"A Middle-Aged Mom's Response to a Daycare Center's Shenanigans." *BRICKrhetoric*. May 2014.

"A Vicious Cycle Partially Fostered by Conks and Other Planar Groupings." *Spark!* Dec. 2012.

"Abetted by a Need to Know." *Bindweed*. Jun. 2016.

"Acquiring Provisions for Pets and Plants." *Winamop*. Sep. 2013.

"Adult Wibbling, Wobbling, Falling Down." *The Scarlet Leaf Review*. Jul. 2018.

"After Twenty Years, Towels Fray." *The Camel Saloon*. 2014.

"Ah, the Aardvark: Classifying Chaos in an Urban Zoo." *Qarrtsiluni*. Apr. 2013.

"All of the Personal Fringes of Prayer." *Spark!* Jun. 2012.

"Along with the Doll." *Spark!* Sep. 2012.

"As a Salute." *Literary Yard*. Mar. 2019.

"As Obsessions Do." *Unsere Winterreise*. Lazarus Media. Jan. 2013. 34-35.

"Asiatic Arecas." *Spark!* Jun. 2015.

"Babes in Buggies" as "Babies in Buggies." *Riverbabble*. Jun. 2014.

"Body, Salubrious: An Unexpected Visitor." *Danse Macabre*. Aug. 2012.

"Can I be Rare, Too?" *Winamop*. Feb. 2020.

"Candy Corn Castles." *Danse Macabre*. Apr. 2013.

"Characters and Old Crocked Pots." *Conceit Magazine*. Aug. 2015.

"Contemporary Coupling." *Mad Swirl*. Apr. 2014.

"Converse." *Fowl Feathered Review*. Jul. 2013. 44.

"Covered with a Leotard." *Mad Swirl*. Apr. 2015.

"Crocus Friends." *Ygdrasil*. Sep. 2013.

"Downpour." *The Cat's Meow*. Jul. 2011.

"Doxing." *Voice of Eve*. Jul. 2019.

"Duplicitous, Bleeding Hearts." *Winamop*. Dec. 2018.

"During Allegorical Surveys." *Danse Macabre*. Apr. 2013.

"Each Elderly Face." *Fowl Feathered Review*. Jul. 2013. 43.

"Falling Cradleless through Spring's Evening Boughs." *Mad Swirl*. Jan. 2013.

"Fernweh." *BlogNostics*. Jul. 2019.

"First Showing." *Riverbabble*. Jan. 2015.

"Flipping Houses." *Voice of Eve*. Jul. 2019.

"Fortuitous Wanderings." *Winamop*. Feb. 2013.

"Generations of Morning Glories: Dialoging a Changing Mother/Daughter Relationship." *Spark!* Sep. 2012.

"Great Veils of Regret" as "Fear Shrouds Me." *Ken*Again*. Sep. 2012. Rpt. *Re/Verse*. Jan. 2013.

"Had I Wishes." *Fluid and Crystallized*. Fowlpox Press. Jun. 2012.

"HaPupakim." *New Bourgeois*. Mar. 2016.

"Her Samurai Sheep's Revenge." *Fowl Feather Review*. Jan. 2014.

"Here, Pingo Sits: [An] Intergalactic Placement of Sentiment." *Winamop*. Feb. 2013.

"Holiday Clothing" as "Procuring and Adjusting Holiday Garments." *Winamop*. May 2013.

"I Gave You Me." *Winamop*. Jul. 2018.

"Juliet Capulet, Her Nurse, and the Moon." *Winamop*. Jul. 2018.

"Kowtowing to Social Fads: A Tragic Romance." *Winamop*. Jul. 2019.

"La! This Joy that is Spring." *Pavilion Magazine*. Mar. 2014.

"Laudanum Tinctures." *Bewildering Stories*. Jan. 2017.

"Like Stars in the Sky." *Winamop*. Aug. 2019.

"Loving One's Chavrusot: Authentic Brotherhood Evidenced at a Wedding," *Ygdrasil*. May 2013.

"Matters of Men Rea." *Literary Yard*. Mar. 2019.

"Measured Anguish at the Local Toadstool Malt Shop: Take Two" as "The Local Toadstool Malt Shop Revisited." *Pink. Girl. Ink.* Jul. 2017.

"Midas' Touch." *Fluid and Crystallized*. Fowlpox Press. Jun. 2012.

"Munchkins Wearing Braids: A High School Perspective" as "Munchkins in Braids: A High School Perspective." *Pyrokinection*. Dec. 2012.

"My Mister." *Winamop*. Feb. 2014.

"No More Notice." *Winamop*. Nov. 2017.

"Not Loving the CDC's Word Ban." *Winamop*. Nov. 2019.

"Odd as Cows in Fur-Lined Tress." *Winamop*. Sep. 2018.

"Of Bandoliers and Boulangeries." *Winamop*. Feb. 2020.

"Of That Particular Ilk." *Ygdrasil*. Sep. 2016.

"Or by Inland Lakes." *vox poetica*. Dec. 2017.

"Ostranennie," *Literary Yard*. Mar. 2019.

"Other Olden, 'Logy' Communications." *Winamop*. Nov. 2019.

"Paper and Kindred Devices." *Danse Macabre*. Apr. 2013.

"Passing Thoughts." *Winamop*. Sep. 2012.

"Patterning with Holes." *Spark!* Sep. 2013.

"Peach Pit Bridges." *Spark!* Feb. 2014.

"Personal Journeys." *Les Femmes Folles*. Mar. 2016.

"Pigeons in Oakland." *Chanticleer*. Apr. 2013.

"Pleasant Wishes, Little Kisses." *Winamop*. Feb. 2013.

"Pregnant with Joy." *Spark!* Sep. 2013.

"Prioritizing Quintessential Deeds." *vox poetica*. Sep. 2017.

"Proportional Verse." Etc: *A Review of General Semantics*. Jan. 2013.

"Puppy Dogs and Feral Cats: An Urban Beddy-Bye." *Winamop*. Nov. 2014.

"Racing Bikes." *Gypsy Daughter's Brown Bagazine*. Jun. 2011. 17.

"Reluctant to Use Their Words." *Winamop*. Jun. 2014.

"Returning to Egypt with a Clean Lute." *The Camel Saloon*. Feb. 2014.

"Rubbernecking from Bus Stops." *Bewildering Stories*. Feb. 2019.

"Sail Away." *Winamop*. May 2015.

"Salivating Away Tension." *Pink. Girl. Ink.* Sep. 2015.

"Savta's Bijou." *Mad Swirl*. Jul. 2017. Rpt. *The Best of Mad Swirl 2017*. Mad Swirl. Jun. 2018.

"Scurrilous." *Bewildering Stories*. Oct. 2018.

"Select Taxons of Behavior." *Winamop*. Aug. 2019.

"Seltzer and Other Social Signifiers." *Winamop*. Feb. 2014.

"September." *Winamop*. Jul. 2013.

"Shedding." *The Camel Saloon*. Dec. 2011.

"Shrewdness Derived from an Excess of Disquiet." *Tuck Magazine*. Aug. 2017.

"Silver Moss Fingers." *vox poetica*. Sep. 2013.

"Sneering at Womanizing Linguistics." *Bewildering Stories*. Feb. 2017.

"So Aloes Grew." *Fluid and Crystallized*. Fowlpox Press. Jun. 2012.

"Some Boats." *Winamop*. Jul. 2018.

"Starlight." *Winamop*. Sep. 2013.

"Superiors' Specifications." *Winamop*. Nov. 2019.

"Swimming in Shamayim: Jacob Nissim Bensussen." *Remembering Yaakov*. Mar. 2010. Rpt. *Fluid and Crystallized*. Fowlpox Press. Jun. 2012.

"Teenage Infatuation." *Winamop*. Feb. 2020.

"That Photo, Which She Carried to Class." *Zingara Poetry*. Dec. 2016.

"The Basis for Evil Machinations." *SAND Journal*. May 2016. 62-63.

"The Mage's Incomplete Solace." *Winamop*. Jun. 2018.

"The Physical that was You." *vox poetica*. May 2013.

"The Real Thing." *The Medulla Review*. Nov. 2012.

"The Sanctity of Lists." *Really System*. Apr. 2014.

"The Ways in Which We Puttered." *Literary Yard*. Jun. 2018.

"The Willing Face of Corporate Chemistry." *Mad Swirl*. Jun. 2018.

"Those Intricate Pastel Patterns." *The Camel Saloon*. May 2013.

"Tomorrow's Bleak, Worry-Woven Landscape." *Winamop*. Nov. 2017.

"Twinkle Stinking Little Star." *Dancing with Hedgehogs*. Fowlpox Press. 2014.

"Underrated as Crummy Texts." *Ygdrasil*. Sep. 2014.

"Unlike the Teenage Attitude Attributed to the Prime Minister's Dalliance." *Literary Hatchet*. May 2013.

"Voguing with Current Federal Bureaucrats." *Mad Swirl*. Feb.2015.

"Welkin." *The Voices Project*. Jan. 2019.

"When Adopting Great Danger." *Winamop*. Feb. 2018.

"Whether Equine or Strigine." *Bewildering Stories*. Jan. 2020.

"Whispers of Wilderness." *vox poetica*. Dec. 2013.

Acknowledgements:

The kindnesses I have received from members of the writing community have not been random; they have been intentional as well as have been fashioned for my needs. It remains the case that I cherish each and every supportive relationship formed with my fellow writers and editors. I would be shouting into the wind, spitting on myself, or otherwise losing the value inherent in patterning bits and pieces of nuance without these folks. Said differently, I remain indebted to the good women and men, who cheer me on, who tell me when my work seems lacking, or who otherwise help me grow as a writer.

About the Author:

KJ Hannah Greenberg, who used to teach rhetoric and sociology, abandoned staid discourse for more wonky ways of moving text around pages. These days, Hannah enjoys watching dust bunnies breed beneath her sofa and becomes preoccupied when attempting to matchmake word pairs like "balderdash" with "xylophone" or "twaddle" with "elated." Known to have more attitude than any sheep-deprived Komodo dragon, Hannah fashions whole or otherwise bitten writing and then allows it to flutter through global venues. Ever incorrigible, she makes her prickle of imaginary hedgehogs line up in pairs (however, sylvan creatures to a one, they, subsequently, construct narratives from leaves, shiny bugs, and marshmallow fluff.)

Hannah's been nominated four times for the Pushcart Prize in Literature, once for the Million Writers Award, and once for The Best of the Net. She has received National Endowment for the Humanities monies, too. Currently, Hannah serves as an Associate Editor at *Bewildering Stories*. Her greatest ambition, nonetheless, remains a full night's sleep.

KJ Hannah Greenberg's Other Books

Prose

The Nexus of the Sun, the Moon, and Mother (Seashell Books, 2020)
Walnut Street (Bards & Sages Publishing, 2019)
Whistling for Salvation (Seashell Books, 2019)
On Golden Limestone (Seashell Books, 2018)
Rhetorical Candy (Seashell Books, 2018)
Concatenation (Bards and Sages Publishing, 2018)
Tosh: Select Trash and Bosh of Creative Writing (Crooked Cat Books, 2017)
My Neighbor Judy (Tachlis Magazine. 2017-2018)
Dreams are for Coloring Books: Midlife Marvels (Seashell Books, 2017)
Can I Be Rare, Too? (Bards and Sages Publishing, 2017)
Ten Kilo and One Million (Crooked Cat Books, 2017)
Friends and Rabid Hedgehogs (Bards and Sages Publishing, 2016)
Jerusalem Sunrise (Imago Press, 2015)
Word Citizen (Tailwinds Press, 2015)
Cryptids (Bards and Sages Publishing, 2015)
The Immediacy of Emotional Kerfuffles, 2nd ed. (Bards and Sages Publishing, 2015)
Don't Pet the Sweaty Things, 2nd ed. (Bards and Sages Publishing, 2014)
Oblivious to the Obvious: Wishfully Mindful Parenting (French Creek Press, 2010)
Conversations on Communication Ethics (Praeger, 1991)
Watercolors (Scotch & Soda Productions, 1979)

Poetics

The Wife/Mom (Seashell Books, 2019)
Beast There—Don't That (Fomite Press, 2019)
Mothers Ought to Utter Only Niceties (Unbound CONTENT, 2017)
A Grand Sociology Lesson (Lit Fest Press, 2016)
Dancing with Hedgehogs (Fowlpox Press, 2014)
The Little Temple of My Sleeping Bag (Dancing Girl Press, 2014)
Citrus-Inspired Ceramics (Aldrich Press, 2013)
Intelligence's Vast Bonfires (Lazarus Media, 2012)
Supernal Factors (The Camel Saloon Books on Blog, 2012)
Fluid & Crystallized (Fowlpox Press, 2012)
A Bank Robber's Bad Luck with His Ex-Girlfriend (Unbound CONTENT, 2011)

www.ingramcontent.com/pod-product-compliance
Lightning Source LLC
Chambersburg PA
CBHW081938160726
47999CB00008B/2430

* 9 7 9 8 6 2 2 9 4 0 7 4 3 *